# A Little Word From Us

When Jinny said 6 weeks ago shall we refresh the book and put some new stuff in it, I said okay. 6 weeks later and here we are with a completely new book. Are we mad? I think so. Has it been a baking frenzy and chaos? Yes it has. Did my bin turn into the cake disaster monster? Yes it did. Would we do it any other way??? I'd rather not answer that, but with that being said I tend to work better under pressure. Although I think it was me that wanted the book to be ready in time to launch for November, I will take the blame.

So for 6 weeks my other half Russ, our dog Dio and our new puppy Connie Cupcake have had to put up with the kitchen over run with baking products, goodies, and equipment, me being tired and grumpy, especially on days where nothing goes right (we all have them). Yesterday I was happy to put all the baking equipment away in the pantry and resume some kind of normality. Will we do it again? Probably!

So after many experiments, trials, taste testing, and feeding my family, friends and neighbours, we are finally finished.

I have thoroughly enjoyed this journey, writing book number 2 with Jinny, we both learned so much last time and have used that to our advantage. I'm so happy that Jinny is the tech genius of us both, give me a spreadsheet any day. She has done us proud, editing and putting the recipes together, with me bugging her and asking for ridiculous requests and bright colours that she hates. For this I apologise!

Our fantastic Facebook group is an absolute inspiration to us, we have amazing bakers and artists as members, with so much shared knowledge and such a kind and inspiring bunch, we couldn't do this without you all. Every comment, like and share, means such a lot, thank you all so much.

I think we now need a few days to relax, and catch up on things.

Is that the wine fridge calling me? Yes it is!!

Love Jo

Well Well Well JO, what can I say, here we are we have done it. Wowwww I am surprised I am still married, my hubby has spent more time with the checkout lady at Tesco, than he has with me. Im sure they were very concerned with the amount of butter and eggs he was buying!! My bin has been the same, there were 3 solid days where everything went wrong. Cakes sank and I don't mean a little, I actually think it's a talent. The bit I am most concerned about is that even though I am stood watching the sinkhole get deeper and deeper, I still wait for the timer to go off before removing it from the oven!! What did I think was going to happen, these cakes would have needed industrial scaffolding to stay up, but I obviously thought the cool air would fix it!!!!

There has been lots of laughter, near tears, frustration and swearing, but you don't remember it until you're stuck back in the moment again, like child birth!!

I really hope you enjoy this book, we are super proud of it and I even like the colours!!

For each of you that has purchased this book thank you so so much. There would be no Jinny & Jo without your support.

**Love Jinny**

# JINNY & JO'S
# TOP TIPS

## Ingredients

Milk Powder...... this is the powder you put into coffee, so you will find it in the hot beverage section of the supermarket. It add a creaminess without adding extra liquid and also stabilises a bake.

Golden Caster Sugar..... This gives a lovely subtle caramel flavour but holds the structure of caster sugar that is needed. If you do not have this then you can weigh out the full amount of caster sugar and then remove 2 tablespoons, then replace them with light brown sugar.

Buttermilk..... To make this, cos let's face it, who uses a whole carton!!!! Add 250g/ml full fat milk into a bowl and add with 1 tsp of lemon juice or white wine/cider vinegar to it. Leave this for 10 mins and it will have curdled into buttermilk.

Eggs.....We always use large eggs unless otherwise stated, large eggs are approx 65g per egg and medium are approx 55g per egg. We weigh them in their shells.

Full Fat!!!! Can i use Low Fat???
Short answer no, unfortunately you would think you can, but the fats that are in the milk/yogurt are essential to make the bake work. Oh the science of cake baking that now fills my brain is insane!!!

Muscavado Sugar...this goes through a different process than the white/brown sugars, so they don't behave the same. Unfortunately you do really need to use this when stated.

# Methods

Eggs**.....** To add eggs into your batter, follow these steps
Use room temperature eggs, if you store them in the fridge take them out a few hours before use.
Add them one by one.
Pour each egg into the batter, whisk it in on a low speed, once you see it incorporating, turn the speed up to medium for around 10 seconds. It should look silky. Do this with all of the eggs needed.
If it does curdle the flour will pull it all in together.

Room Temperature Butter.... What is it!!!!!!
Who knows, in the UK/Ireland room temp in the winter is 3/4C and in the summer 25C!!!!
So how do we achieve it...
Melt the butter, but then it splits altering the bake, so no.
Put it under a warm glass, but then the outside splits and it's hard in the middle, so no.
Take it out and leave it on the side in the winter, well that's gonna take months, so again no.
It all gets very frustrating.
So our way...... Remember Connors Buttercream, we melt the butter through a very controlled process. This melts the butter to a useable consistency, without splitting or affecting the structure of the butter. This whips up with the sugar beautifully and makes life so much easier... Give it a try!!!
You don't want your butter to go florescent, this means it is splitting. It should always look the colour of custard. In colder countries, or if it is in the fridge and you know it won't melt. Pop it cubed up into the microwave straight from the fridge and turn it on for 5 seconds, then stir and do another 5 seconds again, repeat this cycle until it resembles thick custard. This is around 25-27C (77-80F). This is essentially the Connors Method without the Icing sugar on page 146
I hope this helps, it is such a confusing, frequently asked about subject.

My Bowl Is TOO Cold!!..... We have all been there you put your "room temp" butter into the bowl whip it up but it just sticks to the sides AAAHHHHH. To solve this boil the kettle and pour the water int the mixing bowl, swish it around the sides and pour it straight out. It should not be in the bowl for more than 5 seconds. Give the bowl a dry and it should be warm to the touch, NOT hot, you can leave it to cool if it feels too hot. Once you can only feel a slight temperature add in the butter and whip. Magic! it whips up beautifully. Use this for batter and buttercream.

# Our Amazing "Simply Colours"

## We have 3 Ranges in our Colours

### Connors Buttercream Silk

Our Connors Buttercream Silk Range is perfect for Fondant, Royal Icing & Buttercreams. We recommend complimenting the colours using our Connors Buttercream Silk recipe, although they do work amazingly with all your favourite buttercreams. By amending the amount of colouring you use, these are perfect for both subtle and the more vibrant shades.

Gel Food Colours

Vegan Friendly

Gluten Free

Whilst we have used Connors in Chocolate and it did perform well, this is not its intended use and may not come upto the same standards as the Intense/Candy Range.

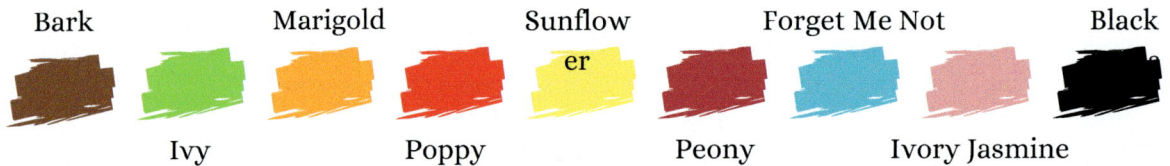

| Bark | | Marigold | | Sunflower | | Forget Me Not | | Black |
|---|---|---|---|---|---|---|---|---|
| | Ivy | | Poppy | | Peony | | Ivory Jasmine | |

### Caandy Colours

Our Candy Colour Range is perfect for Fondants, Chocolate, and Buttercreams, we recommend using our amazing Connors Buttercream Silk, but they work with all varieties of buttercream. These are also perfect for colouring chocolate and modeling chocolate.

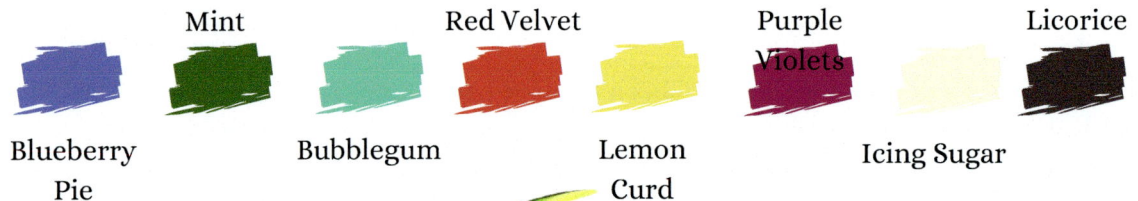

| | Mint | | Red Velvet | | Purple Violets | | Licorice |
|---|---|---|---|---|---|---|---|
| Blueberry Pie | | Bubblegum | | Lemon Curd | | Icing Sugar | |

**LCO Trading LTD**

**ALL AVAILABLE FROM**     **LCO TRADING UK**

International Shipping Available

# Intense Colours

Our Intense Colour Range is perfect for Fondants, Chocolate, and Buttercreams, we recommend using our amazing Connors Buttercream Silk, but they work with all varieties of buttercream. These are also perfect for colouring chocolate and modeling chocolate.
These are gel based colours.

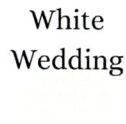

Purple Rain

Blue Moon

White Wedding

Spirit In The Sky

Red Red Wine

Greensleves

I know we are biased but these colours are of an amazing quality, with only a small amount you can achieve those bright and vibrant colours
you need, to showcase all your hard work.

ALL AVAILABLE FROM **LCO** Trading LTD LCO TRADING UK

International Shipping Available

# Why We Bake!

Baking, oh glorious baking! It's not just about meticulously measuring ingredients and religiously following a recipe. No, no, my dear friends, it's so much more. Baking is an adventure that takes you on a wild ride, with twists and turns that would make even the bravest of souls tremble. Imagine this: you enter your kitchen with all the grace of a ballerina (singing delicately!!), armed with a spatula in one hand and a whisk in the other. As you start measuring, chaos unfolds. Flour goes airborne like a snowstorm, butter somehow ends up on the ceiling, and eggs dance precariously on the edge of the counter, threatening to take a leap of faith. But wait, it doesn't end there. Oh no.. Baking has a way of turning your kitchen into a hot mess. Cupboards fill up with gadgets and gizmos that you once believed were essential. Suddenly, you have three different types of cake pans, ten different types of spatulas, and a contraption that claims it can perfectly smooth a cake within a minute!! You look back at your innocent self, who thought all you needed was a mixing bowl and a trusty oven. Oh, how naïve you were.

And let's not forget those moments when things do go wrong. Baking has a way of turning even the calmest of individuals into demons. Burnt cookies, sunken cakes, and caramel that turns into an unbreakable toffee fortress, if you even manage to get it that hard. The frustration builds up, the sweet treats become the enemy, and before you know it, you're shouting words that would make even Gordon Ramsay blush. Baking can make Dr. Jekyll morph into the monstrous Mr. Hyde, all in the pursuit of culinary greatness.

But fear not, my fellow bakers, for amidst the chaos, there lies a glimpse of hope. A ray of light that promises redemption. Because when all the flour has settled and the smoke alarms have ceased their shrill serenade, there it stands: a masterpiece of pure love and sheer passion.

That cake with its fluffy layers and decadent frosting is your triumphant creation, it's a testament to your resilience and determination, despite the possible, hidden not-so-glorious journey it took to get there!!!!!

# USEFUL INFO

## Socials

You can find us on most social media platforms.....needy right!!!
So where are we??

We have a Facebook Page, where we do Lives and share recipes and videos. This is called "Baking it Simple with Jinny and Jo"

Our Facebook group, where we have a chat with our members and give discounts. This is a really fun, interactive group. This is caked "Baking With Jinny & Jo Community group"

Instagram, you will find us under "Jinny & Jo"

TikTok, again "Jinny & Jo"

YouTube "Baking With Jinny and Jo"

Our Website is also "Baking With Jinny & Jo"

### Our Amazon StoreFront.

If you search "Baking With Jinny & Jo" Amazon on Google, we will pop straight up. Here you will see all the products we use & are needed for baking and decorating in one easy place.

**From Cake tins to Flower Decorating We Have you Covered**

## Recommendations

### Callebaut
We always use Callebaut Chocolate. The quality and taste is amazing, bringing your bakes up to the next level.
We would recommend

White Chocolate W2
Milk Chocolate 823
Dark Chocolate 811
Gold, a beautiful caramel flavour.
Ruby, a fruity flavour with citrus undertones.
Plein Arome, a hugely decadent chocolate flavour

### Wexford Home Preserves

For those of you that don't have the time to make homemade jam, but wish you did, Wexford Home Preserves have got you covered. Wexford Home Preserves is an artisan maker of multiple award winning jams, marmalades, savoury preserves and speciality preserves.

# Contents

# CUPCAKES

Unless other wise stated our recipes will make 12 cupcakes. Check the size of your cases, some "cupcake" cases are really for fairy cakes and will be very small. I tend to use "muffin" cases as then I know they will be the size I am looking for.

Do your cases peel?? some just do and it's so annoying. One reason why they maybe doing this is due to condensation, so leaving them in the tin for too long. When they are cool enough to remove, place them onto a cooling rack. Also try the rice trick, place a few grains of rice in the bottom of the tin hole!! (you know what I mean!!) before adding your cases, this will absorb any excess oils.

Do your cupcakes bake unevenly!! turn off that fan setting, it makes a huge difference. I no longer bake cupcakes with the fan on.

How do I fill them!!
There are many ways to get them all the same size, use a piping bag, but cut a large enough hole so that your not squeezing the batter out, affecting the lovely air in those cupcakes. Now bare with me this does make sense......to me!! Count whilst you pipe the batter in. This way you will put the same amount in each case, eg 1,2,3 and repeat!!!
Cookie Scoop, you can buy these on our Amazon Store Front, the large ones, these are great too. A heaped dessert spoon, or you could weigh each one!!!
How do you know when they are baked?
NEVER break the seal across the top unless you are pretty confident they are nearly done, this will cause them to drop. They need the baked structure to keep them up.
Using a towel tap the tray, if they wobble they are nowhere near done, shut that door!!
If there is no wobble you can now use a skewer to test them, it should come out clean, crumbs are fine!!

# Cupcakes

# CHOCOLATE CUPCAKES

## Ingredients

175g Plain Flour

1/2 tsp Baking Powder

1/2 Tsp Bicarbonate of Soda

⅛ Tsp Salt

150g Caster Sugar

100g Light Brown Sugar

55g Cocoa Powder

125g Cooled Boiled Water ( I use grams for my liquids)

50g Vegetable Oil

50g Melted Butter

2 Large eggs approx 130g

1 Tsp Vanilla

2 Tbsp Buttermilk ( you can make this with 2tbsp milk and 1/4tsp lemon juice or vinegar. wait for 10 mins until curdled, its then ready to use)

## Method

Pre-Heat your oven to 170C/150C Fan/Gas 3/325F and pop your liners into your muffin tin.

Combine the flour, bicarb, baking powder, salt, sugars & cocoa together until incorporated.

In another bowl whisk together your water, oil, melted butter, eggs, vanilla & buttermilk.

Place your dry, mixed ingredients into your bowl (you can use a stand mixer or do this one by hand, it's so super easy) and gradually stir in your wet, until all the two have fully incorporated.

Pour this into a jug, as the batter is very wet and tip evenly into the cases. I fill mine approx ¾ full.

Place into the oven for 19-22 minutes depending on your oven these times may vary. Grab a cup of tea and ask someone else to do the washing up!!! (it's worth a try)

Cupcakes will be done when there is no wobble and a toothpick comes out clean.

After 3 minutes remove from the tin and cool on a rack.

# VANILLA CUPCAKES

## Ingredients

190g Plain Flour
190g Caster Sugar
1 1/2 Tsp Baking Powder
1/8 Tsp Salt
115g "Room Temp" Unsalted Butter
105g Full Fat Plain Yogurt
4 Eggs
2 Tsp Vanilla Extract

## Method

Pre-Heat your oven to 180C/160CFan/350F/Gas 4 and line your tin with muffin cases.

Separate your eggs and keep the yolks and and whites in separate bowls. Divide the sugar into 2 bowls.

Clean out your mixing bowl with some lemon juice or vinegar to remove any grease. Then pour in the egg white and begin whipping with the balloon whisk, on low/medium for a minute. Turn it up to medium/high and once you see the egg white has become all foamy, begin adding in the sugar you divided in half earlier (keep the other half for the batter). Only add in the sugar slowly or it will deflate your beautiful (hopefully!!) meringue. Now turn it up to high and it will be done when the balloon whisk fills up with the meringue, and you can tip the bowl upside down, without having to clean the floor!!!Pour this into another bowl, give the mixer bowl a clean and we will begin the batter.

We will be using the reverse method, so add the flour, baking powder, salt, and the other half of the sugar you set aside, into the bowl along with the butter. Using a paddle attachment whip this all together starting on slow (as the flour will cover you!!) and build up. It may go just past the breadcrumb stage and begin merging together!! To this add in the yogurt and vanilla, give it a slight mix and with the mixer on low, then add in the egg yolks in one at a time. When this is all combined it is time to add the meringue.

Fold in the meringue gently this may take a few minutes, once it is all combined spoon the mix into the muffin cases. You need to fill the cases just over 3/4 these don't rise as much as regular cupcakes. They do slightly deflate a little upon cooling. I left around a cm gap from the top. Pop them in the oven, for cupcakes I highly recommend NOT using the fan setting, you will get a much more even, and better bake. Mine took 20 mins.

Cool them on a baking rack, once cool you can top them with Vanilla Buttercream on page 146

# STRAWBERRIES & CREAM CUPCAKES

## Ingredients

### Cupcakes

185g Plain Flour
185g Unsalted Butter
175g Caster Sugar
35g Freeze Dried
Strawberries
(Crushed into crumb,
use a rolling pin &
ziplock)
3 LG Eggs
Pinch Salt
1/2 tsp Baking Powder
1/2 tsp Bicarbonate of Soda
2 tsp Milk Powder
( the kind you put in your
coffee)
1 tsp Vanilla Extract
1 Tbsp Milk
Food Colouring if required

### Filling

1 Tbsp Strawberry Jam
(I use *Wexford Home
Preserves*/ or you can
make your own on *page
144*
2 Tbsp Icing Sugar
1 tsp Milk Powder

## Method

Begin by filling your cupcake tray with liners and pre heating your oven to:
150C/170CFan/325F/Gas 3

### Cupcakes

Add room temp butter with the sugar/milk powder/colouring (optional) and crumbed, freeze dried strawberries to the mixer. Whip for around 2 mins until light and fluffy, scraping down half way.

If you struggle with your butter sticking to the sides, pour boiling water into the mixing bowl first, then pour is straight out. This will slightly heat the sides, preventing the butter from sticking.

Now add ALL the remaining cupcake ingredients and mix together, on medium for 30 seconds, scrape down ensuring you get right to the bottom of the bowl, and then a final 30 second mix.

To pour into the cupcake tins, I put my batter into a piping bag, this allows me to be able to control the amount in each case. I count/sing 1,2,3 on each so that they are equal!!!!! You know you can imagine me doing it!!!

Make sure your hole in the bag around an inch thick, or the batter will need to be squeezed out and this will affect the air you have produced to make a light sponge.

# Method Continued

Bake these for 19-20 mins so that a skewer comes out clean. Crumbs are ok, sticky batter isn't!!
If you struggle like I do with uniformity through your bake, change your oven setting, turn off the fan and use the 170C, try it I do it all the time now.

## Filling

Spoon your jam into a bowl, give it a mix and try to remove any large bits as they will affect your piping. Now pour in over the icing sugar and milk powder. Once it is all mixed together pop it into the microwave and heat this mixture slightly and give it a final stir. Cover with cling and pop it to one side.
You only need to warm it, this helps it to all come together better and dissolves the powders. So 20 to 30 secs is fine.

Pair with Connors Strawberry Buttercream on Page 148

## Assembly

Pipe the filling we set aside earlier into the cupcakes. Do this placing the jam mix into a piping bag and cut a half a cm hole at the bottom. Now make 4/5 holes in the top of the cupcake using a skewer or lollipop stick. Place the piping bag into the holes and squeeze out some of the mix. Don't add too much, or you will get just a mouthful of jam!! the amount you have will fill 12 cupcakes.
Pipe on the Buttercream, I used a 1M and then I added an additional freeze dried strawberry into the top of each.

# CHOCOLATE TRUFFLE CUPCAKES

Such a beautiful and decadent cupcake, if you love chocolate, you will love these.

## Ingredients

200g soft butter or baking spread (make sure it is super soft)

260g Caster Sugar

2 Eggs

160g Flour

50g Cocoa powder

1 tsp Baking Powder

10 tbsp Milk

1 tsp Vanilla

12 Milk Chocolate Truffles  page 134

1/2 Batch of our Swiss Meringue Buttercream (page 154)

## Method

Preheat the oven to 170C/150CFan/325F/Gas3

In a stand mixer or with a hand mixer, pop all of the ingredients in a bowl and mix until almost combined, stop and scrape down the bowl and the beater and mix again until you have a smooth batter.

Transfer to a prepared cupcake pan with cases and place one truffle on top of each cupcake and bake for 20 to 23 minutes, the top will crack a little and they will bounce back when pushed.

Remove from the tin straight away and cool on a rack.

When the cupcakes are cooled, decorate with Vanilla Swiss meringue buttercream. These are so chocolaty they really benefit from a non chocolate buttercream.

# GINGER & WHITE CHOCOLATE BUTTERCREAM CUPCAKES

These are a super intense ginger flavour and a nod to a favourite winter coffee.

## Ingredients

85g Golden Syrup
115g Black Treacle
100g Butter
215g Caster sugar
1 tsp of Vanilla Extract
125g Milk
2 Large Eggs
265g Plain Flour
4 tsp Ground Ginger
1 tsp Ground Cinnamon
1/4 Tsp Ground Allspice
1 tsp Bicarbonate of Soda
1 tsp Baking Powder

1 Batch of Connors White Chocolate Buttercream

## Method

Preheat the oven to 170 C Fan.

Prepare your cupcake tin with cases.

Melt in a pan the butter, syrup, and treacle, until the butter is melted, you don't want to boil this.

Decant to a bowl and add in the sugar, vanilla and milk. When this is cool enough, not hotter than 30 C you can whisk in the eggs.

Once the eggs are incorporated add in all the dry ingredients and fold together, give it a good mix with a spatula.

Spoon into the cupcake cases up to about 3/4 full.

Bake on the middle shelf for 18 minutes or until a skewer comes out clean.

Top with Connors White Chocolate Buttercream.

Enjoy these on a cold winters day with a hot chocolate or coffee.

# LIME MERINGUE CUPCAKES

These are delicious and amazingly soft and delicate. If you love a meringue pudding you will love these.

## Ingredients

200g soft butter or baking spread (make sure it is super soft)
200g Caster Sugar
60g Lime Curd (recipe is in the book if you can't find a shop bought)
2 Eggs
200g Flour
1 tsp Baking Powder
6 tbsp Milk
1 tsp Vanilla

1/2 Batch of our 7 minute Frosting
**page 153**

## Method

Preheat the oven to 150 C Fan.

In a stand mixer or with a hand mixer, pop all of the ingredients in a bowl and mix until almost combined, stop and scrape down the bowl and the beater and mix again until you have a smooth batter.

Yes its that simple!

Transfer to a prepared cupcake pan with cases and bake for 22 to 25 minutes or until a skewer comes out clean.

Remove from the tin straight away and cool on a rack.

When the cupcakes are cooled, pop some curd into a piping bag and force a whole the centre of the cupcake with a knife. Put the tip of the bag into the cupcake and squeeze in the curd, you will see the cupcake expand and crack a little on the top, pipe another dollop of curd on the top.

Using a nice piping tip like a 2E, pipe the 7 minute frosting into swirls on the cupcakes.

These will set as they are at room temperature or you can use a kitchen blow torch to brown the tops of the frosting, my favourite part, I'm a bit of a pyromaniac.

# SUPER FLUFFY LEMON CUPCAKES

## Ingredients

180g Plain Flour
1 1/2 tsp Baking Powder
110g Softened Butter (not melted)
4 Large Eggs
100g Plain Yogurt
Zest of 3 Lemons
2 tbsp Lemon Juice
180g Caster Sugar
Pinch of Salt

## Method

Pre-Heat your oven to 180C/160CFan/350F/Gas 4 and line your tin with muffin cases.

Separate your eggs and keep the yolks and and whites separate. Divide the sugar into 2 bowls.

Clean out your mixing bowl with some lemon juice or vinegar to remove any grease. Then pour in the egg white and begin whipping with the balloon whisk, on low/medium for a minute. Turn it up to medium/high and once you see the egg white has become all foamy, begin adding the sugar you divided in half earlier (keep the other half for the batter). Only add in the sugar slowly or it will deflate your beautiful (hopefully!!) meringue. Now turn it up too high and it will be done when the balloon whisk fills up with the meringue, and you can tip the bowl upside down, without having to clean the floor!!!Pour this into another bowl, give the mixer bowl a clean and we will begin the batter.

We will be using the reverse method, so add the flour, baking powder, salt, lemon zest, and the other half of the sugar you set aside, into the bowl along with the butter. Using a paddle attachment whip this all together starting on slow (as the flour will cover you!!) and build up. It may go just past the breadcrumb stage and begin merging together!! To this add in the yogurt and lemon juice, give it a slight mix and with the mixer on low, add in the egg yolks one at a time. When this is all combined it is time to add the meringue.

Fold in the meringue gently this may take a few minutes, once it is all combined spoon the mix into the muffin cases. You need to fill the cases just over 3/4 these don't rise as much as regular cupcakes. They do slightly deflate a little upon cooling. I left around a cm gap from the top.

Pop them in the oven, for cupcakes I highly recommend NOT using the fan setting, you will get a much more even, and better bake. Mine took 20 mins. Cool them on a baking rack, once cool you can top them with ***Lemon Buttercream on page 148***

# CRÈME BRÛLÉ CUPCAKES

## Ingredients

### Cupcakes

220g Plain Flour
20g Cornflour
250g Caster Sugar
1 1/2 tsp Baking Powder
1/4 tsp Salt
80g Soft Butter
100g Buttermilk
90g Milk
1/2 tsp Vanilla Paste
2 Large Eggs

### Cheats Crème Diplomat
#### 1st Part
500g Ready Made Custard
1 1/2 tsp Cornflour
1 tbsp Milk
1/2 tsp Vanilla Paste
25g Cold Butter
#### 2nd Part
230g Double Cream
1 1/2 tsp Milk Powder
1 tbsp Icing Sugar

### Caramel
300g Sugar
50g Water

## Method

To Make the first part of the Creme Diplomat, pop the ready made custard into a pan, mix the cornflour and milk together in a bowl. Turn on a medium heat to the custard and whisk in the cornflour, milk slurry and Vanilla paste. Gently heat this stirring continuously until you see a few bubbles and the mix has thickened, mix in the cold butter. Transfer to a cool bowl or if you want it to cool faster pour it onto a baking sheet. Cover the top of the custard directly with cling film to avoid a skin from forming. Allow this to cool completely.

To make the cupcakes, pop cupcake/muffin cases into a 12 hole pan and preheat the oven to 180C/160CF/350F/Gas4
In a mixer with the paddle attachment, add in all the dry ingredients including the sugar and the butter, set the mixer on low and let this combine to a sandy texture.
Pop the buttermilk and milk into a jug and microwave for about 30 seconds to bring this to about 30 degrees Centigrade. Check that it isn't too hot and add in the vanilla and eggs, whisk this all together.

With the mixer on low slowly pour in two thirds of the wet, not too fast as you want this to incorporate slowly to get an even batter. Stop the mixer and scrape down the paddle and the bowl well. Turn this mixer back onto low and again slowly add the remaining wet mix so that the it incorporates without lumps. After another scrape down, turn the mixer onto medium and beat for about 20 seconds.

Fill the cupcake wrappers to 3/4 full and bake for 22 to 24 minutes or until a skewer comes out clean.

Remove from the tray as soon as they are cooked and cool on a rack until they are completely cold.

Creme Diplomat Part 2. When the custard is cold, whip up the double cream, milk powder and icing sugar until you have firm peaks, careful not to over whip.
Mix up the custard, and the fold in a third of the cream, then repeat this until it is all incorporated and smooth cover and chill until you are ready to use.

To make the caramel, you will need a heavy based saucepan, a thermometer, a pastry brush and small bowl of water, a heat proof silicone mat and a sink of cold water to crash the heat in the pan when it is ready.

Add the sugar and water to the pan and mix together, pop onto a medium high heat depending on your stove. If you have any sugar that has settled on the wall of the pan, use your pastry brush and water to brush around the edges so that the sugar drops down. You need to boil this taking extra care as it will be very hot. If you see any crystals forming around the edges then use the water and brush to wash them down without touching the caramel. Do not stir the caramel.

Using your thermometer you will need to heat this to between 179 and 185 degree's centigrade or until you have a deep straw colour. When your caramel is ready, place the base of the pan very carefully into the bowl of water to crash the temperature down to about 125 degrees centigrade.

With a large spoon you can spoon pools of the caramel onto your silicone mat. It's best to have the mat in a metal tray to be safe and avoid any spillage as the mix is still extremely hot. Do not touch the pools until the caramel has completely cooled.

To assemble, Cut out the top off the cupcake, like you would if you are making fairy cakes, and discard for snacks. Fill a piping bag with the crème diplomat and cut the tip to about a 2 cm hole. With the bag upright pipe the cream onto the top of the cake pushing down so that it spreads evenly. Do this to all cakes.

Decorate with the disc of caramel or break the caramel into pieces and sprinkle on top.

These are best served straight away. Enjoy!

# COOKIE DOUGH CUPCAKES

## Ingredients

200g Unsalted Butter
190g Plain Flour
1 Tbsp Corn Flour
100g Caster Sugar
100g Light Brown Sugar
1 Tbsp Milk Powder
1/2 Tsp Bicarbonate of Soda
1/2 Tsp Baking Powder
1/8 Tsp Salt
3 Large Eggs
2 Tsp Vanilla Extract
3 Tbsp Full Fat Yogurt
185g Chopped Cookies **page 110**

## Method

Pre Heat your oven to 170C/150CFan/325F/Gas3
Line your cupcake tin with muffin/cupcake cases.

Begin by chopping up your cookies into pieces, I chop mine to around 1-2cm thick.

Into your mixer place your sugars and "room Temp" butter. Give these a whip up for a few minutes until it becomes all light and fluffy.

Into this add your eggs, vanilla & yogurt. Don't mix them yet.... Hold it!

In a separate bowl mix together your flour, bicarb, baking powder, salt & milk powder. Give these a mix up and then pour it onto the rest of the ingredients in the mixer. Now you can whip, whip, whip these up until the batter is all smooth and fully incorporated. Scrape down half way through, you shouldn't mix for longer than a minute.

Remove the bowl from the stand.

In a bowl cover your cookies with the corn flour and give them a mix around. ( this will help them to stick in the batter and not fall to the bottom. Fold these into the mix and spoon into your cases. Fill them 3/4 full.

Bake for 21-23 mins, once cool enough to touch, transfer them to a cooling rack.

Enjoy these alone or top with a vanilla or chocolate buttercream **pages 146/150**

# Muffins

# CHOCOLATE MUFFINS

## Ingredients

115g Plain Flour

1tbsp Cornflour

½ tsp Baking Powder

¾ tsp Bicarbonate of Soda

55g Light Brown Sugar

55g Caster Sugar

1/8 tsp Salt

¼ tsp Coffee (Granules or

Powder)

30g Cocoa Powder

60g Butter

75g Full Fat Milk

65g Sour Cream

½ tsp Vanilla Extract

1 Egg

35g Honey

120g Choc Chips

We recommend using

Callebaut

## Method

Preheat oven to 220C/200C Fan/Gas 7/425F. Line your tin with cases (I recommend tulip cases)

Add flour, cornflour, baking powder, bicarb, sugars, cocoa, salt and coffee into your mixing bowl. Give these a good mix around with a spatula.

Cube your butter and place it into your mixing bowl with the dry ingredients. With your spatula, coat the butter in the flour.

On a medium to low speed, mix all of these up on your stand mixer until it resembles breadcrumbs, you can use the whisk or paddle attachment.

Next add all of the wet ingredients into a separate bowl and combine.

Then pour the wet ingredients into the dry, mix on low speed. This creates a lovely rich batter.

Spoon into the tulip cases level with the tin or if cupcake cases, fill just over ¾ full.

CALLEBAUT®
BELGIUM 1911

# CHOCOLATE MUFFINS

Add 20g chocolate chips onto the top of each muffin, and just let them lie there.

Give the tray a bang to level off and place it into the preheated oven.

Bake for 6 minutes, then without opening the oven door reduce the temperature to 190C/170C Fan/Gas 5/375F for another 12 minutes.

*The change in temperature is what causes the classic broken, dome muffin top*

** This mix makes 5 Tulip Cases or 6 Muffin Cases

CALLEBAUT®
BELGIUM 1911

# BANOFFEE MUFFINS

## Ingredients

### Muffins
### Dry
150g Plain Flour

1 Tbsp Corn Flour

1 Tsp Baking Powder

1 Tsp Bicarbonate of Soda

55g Caster Sugar

55g Dark Brown Sugar

### Wet
1 Tsp White Wine/Cider Vinegar

40g Flavourless Oil ( I used Vegetable)

130g Mashed Banana ( I used Blackening Bananas)

65g Milk (Soya if Vegan/Dairy Free)

35g Yogurt (Soya if Vegan/ Dairy Free)

1 Tsp Vanilla Extract

### Toffee Sauce
110g Dark Brown Sugar

100g Salted Butter (I use Flora Vegan Block for Dairy Free)

55g Cream ( I used Alpro Soya Cream for Dairy Free)

1/2 Tsp Vanilla Extract

### Crumble
50g Plain Flour

50g Caster Sugar

35g Butter ( Again Flora Vegan Block for Dairy Free)

Light brown Sugar to sprinkle

# Method

Pre Heat your oven to 220C/200C Fan/425F/Gas 7

Begin by adding your cases to the tin, as the batter needs to go into the oven as soon as it is mixed. This recipe makes 6 muffins, if you have a 12 muffin tin, then use the middle rows and fill the outer holes with boiling water. This will help the muffins rise.

In a bowl add all of your dry ingredients together and give them a good mix. Now set this to one side.

In a separate bowl add all of the wet together and again fully mix together.

Now pour the wet onto the dry. The bicarb will start to react with the vinegar immediately so fold in the mixture fast. If you are doing this by hand DO NOT mix more than 15 times.

This may sound silly but muffins hate being messed with and if they are over mixed they will become rubbery. This can happen very quickly so we need to mix and then fill the cases quickly and gently.

Fill.... tulip cases so that the batter is in line with the tin

Fill.... Cases Just over 3/4 Full. I recommend tulip cases if you can get them.

Place into your Pre heated oven and without opening the door reduce the temperature after 6 mins to 190C/170C Fan/375F/Gas 5 for a further 12 to 14 mins.

Once cooled transfer the muffins onto a cooling rack.

## Toffee

Place all of the ingredients into a saucepan or a frying pan and using a spatula continuously stir until the sauce reaches 110C.

Remove from the heat transfer into a heat proof bowl and cover with cling film to prevent a skin from forming.

Once cool add in the vanilla

## Crumble

Place the flour and sugar into a bowl and pour over the melted butter, mix until it all comes together. Transfer onto a baking sheet and using your hands, push the mixture flat and level. Sprinkle on some brown sugar and place into the preheated oven 200C/180C Fan/400F/Gas 6 for around 6 mins until the edges start going golden brown.

Once this has cooled break it up into crumble and set to one side.

## Assembly

Using a knife or a nozzle core out a centre piece of the muffin, keeping the top.

Place the toffee into a piping bag ( heat in the microwave if it is too thick)

Fill the hole with toffee sauce and place the lid back on. Drizzle some more over the top and smooth it out with a spoon, this will help the crumble to stick.

Now sprinkle the crumble over the top and drizzle with some more toffee....... why not.....

Enjoy

# STICKY TOFFEE PUDDING MUFFINS

## Ingredients

### Muffins
95g Buttermilk
80g Chopped Dried Dates
35g Treacle
1 Large Egg
60g Unsalted Butter
65g Plain Yogurt
130g Plain Flour
30g Corn Flour
3/4 Tsp Bicarbonate of Soda
1/2 Tsp Baking Powder
60g Dark Brown Sugar
50g Caster Sugar

### Toffee Sauce
110g Dark Brown Sugar
100g Salted Butter
55g Cream
1/2 Tsp Vanilla Extract

# Method

## Muffin

Pre-Heat the oven to 220C/200C Fan/425F/Gas 7

Begin by adding your tulip cases to your muffin tin, as the batter needs to go into the oven as soon as it is mixed. This recipe makes 6 muffins, if you have a 12 muffin tin, then use the middle rows and fill the outer holes with boiling water. This will help the muffins rise.

Pour the Buttermilk into a bowl followed by the dried dates. Cover this in clingfilm, then you can either put it into the fridge overnight, or heat it in the microwave for a minute until the dates have softened and incorporated into the buttermilk. Place this to one side.

Add the Flour, Corn flour, Bicarb, Baking Powder, Sugars and Cubed Butter into your mixer. On a low speed begin mixing these together until it all resembles breadcrumbs. ( As the flour begins sticking to the butter you can speed up the mixer)

To this add in your Date Mixture, Egg, Yogurt and Treacle.

Combine all the batter on the lowest speed, only mix until just combined, do not overmix your Muffin batter as it is more temperamental than me!!! ( I'm Ginger its not my fault!!) They can turn very rubbery quickly.

Now immediately spoon the mix into your tulip cases, filling them to the level of the muffin tin. Pop these into the pre heated oven for 6 mins.

After 6 mins without opening the oven door reduce the temperature to 190C/170C Fan/375F/Gas 5 for a further 12 mins.

Once cool transfer to a cooling rack and make the toffee.

## Toffee Sauce

Place all of the ingredients into a saucepan or a frying pan and using a spatula continuously stir until the sauce reaches 110C.

Remove from the heat transfer into a heat proof bowl and cover with cling film to prevent a skin from forming.

Once cool add in the vanilla

Core the centre of the muffins out using a knife or a piping nozzle, keep the removed bit of muffin, don't eat it!!! Put it back!!

Fill the cavity with toffee sauce, replace the cored muffin onto the top and finish with a toffee drizzle.

# RASPBERRY & VANILLA MUFFINS

## Ingredients

140g Plain Flour
20g Corn Flour
1 & 1/4 Tsp Baking Powder
1/2 Tsp Bicarbonate of Soda
100g Caster Sugar
80g Unsalted Room Temp Butter
1 large Egg & 1 Yolk
1 & 1/2 Tsp Vanilla Extract
1/16 Tsp Salt
160g/ml Full Fat Milk (I am so sorry it must be full fat!!)
Any Flavour Jam, I used Raspberry from **Wexford Home Preserves**, but any will be yummy.

# Method

Pre Heat the oven to 220C/200Cfan/Gas 7/425F (I recommend NOT using the fan setting, give it a try!!

Line your Muffin Tins with Tulip Cases and set to one side ready. It is important to have everything ready as the batter should be put into the liners and then the oven immediately. This, as well as the temperature change and not over mixing....a 15 mix maximum, will give you that superb dome.

Into your mixer add the flours, raising agents, salt and "room temperature" cubed butter. Begin by mixing on a low setting so the flour doesn't shoot everywhere!!! as it begins to stick to the butter you can gradually turn up the speed to a maximum of medium. It will be ready once the mixture looks like breadcrumbs.

Now add in the sugars and mix again to incorporate.

In a separate bowl whisk together all the wet ingredients as this makes it easier to incorporate, reducing the final mixing time.

Pour this over the dry ingredients and on the lowest setting, begin mixing.... I count the turns and stop at 15.

Remove from the mixer and check it is all combined, give it a gentle fold if needed. Now add into the tulip cases immediately, filling each around 3/4 full. The sides of the cases will support the growth.

Place into the oven and bake for 10 mins. When the timer goes off, without opening the oven door reduce the temperature to..

190C/170Cfan/Gas 5/375F for a further 9 mins.... don't forget the timer.

Once the 9 mins are up using a skewer or similar, poke through the top of the muffin and see if it comes out clean ( crumbs are fine)

Leave these to rest on a baking tray, you can lift them out of the tin as the cases are high and give the support.

Once cool using a profiterole nozzle (or what I call a long one!!! )in a piping bag, fill the bag with as much jam as you think you need.

You want to push the nozzle in 3 times, in different areas of each muffin. Try not to add too much jam or you are going to just get a mouthful of jam and no muffin. This is why we poke 3 times to distribute it in different areas.

Once finished, to make the drizzle glaze I used a tablespoon of icing sugar and added enough jam to it, until the consistency was good enough to go through a small hole in the piping bag and not too loose to swamp the muffin top. Drizzle over and enjoy.

# RASPBERRY & WHITE CHOCOLATE MUFFINS

## Ingredients

1 Large Egg
45g Unsalted Butter
20g Vegetable/Sunflower Oil
90g Full Fat Yogurt
30g Raspberry Stuff *( page 142)*
120g Plain Flour
50g Caster Sugar
15g Dark Sugar
1 Tbsp Milk Powder
1 Tsp Baking Powder
1/8 Tsp Salt
1Tsp Vanilla Extract
100g White Chocolate **(We recommend Callebaut W2)**

Makes 5 Large Muffins

CALLEBAUT®
BELGIUM 1911

## Method

Pre Heat your oven to
220C/200CFan/425F/Gas7
Line your muffin tin with liners, we
recommend tulip cases

Into your mixing bowl place your flour, sugars,
baking powder, salt & milk powder. Give these
a quick mix around and then on the top place
your "room temp" cubed butter. Begin on a low
speed with the paddle attachment, then
gradually build up to medium. The mix should
resemble breadcrumbs, or sand on the beach
(ohhh if only!!)
In a separate bowl mix together the yogurt,
rasp stuff, egg, oil & vanilla. Mix them together
and then pour this over the "breadcrumb"
mixture. For a very short time mix these
together, say 20 seconds, scrape down and
then 20 seconds more.
Remove the bowl from the mixer and fold in
the white choc chips. Fill each tulip case 3/4 full
and bake for 6 minutes. Once the timer goes
off, without opening the oven reduce the temp
to 190C/170CFan/375F/Gas5 for a further 12-14
mins. A skewer should come out clean, crumbs
are fine! Cool on a rack and enjoy. If they are
not as soft the next day you can give them a
quick warm in the oven or a ping in the
microwave.

# OATY, FRUITY MUFFINS

## Ingredients

1 Large Egg
45g Butter
20g Vegetable//Sunflower Oil
120g Full Fat Yogurt
10g Treacle
1 Tsp Vanilla Extract
60g Plain Flour
60g Oats
1 Tsp Baking Powder
25g Caster Sugar
30g Dark Brown Sugar
1/8 Tsp Salt
75g Chopped Glacier Cherries
100g Rasins

Makes 5 Large Muffins

## Method

Pre Heat your oven to 220C/200CFan/425F/Gas7
Line your muffin tin with liners, we recommend tulip cases.

In a bowl add your butter & treacle, melt these together in the microwave. Now add in your oil, yogurt, egg & vanilla. Make sure you add the egg after the oil and yogurt as this will cool the mix before you add the egg, let's have no scrambled egg here!!!! Mix these together.
Grab another bowl, sorry!! oh that washing up!!!
Into this add the flour, oats, baking powder, sugars, salt & dried fruits, give these good stir and then pour the wet ingredients into this. With a short mix together, remember they are like me on a menopausal day, they don't like being touched!!!!!!!
Fill each tulip case 3/4 full and bake for 6 minutes. Once the timer goes off, without opening the oven reduce the temp to 190C/170CFan/375F/Gas5 for a further 12-14 mins. A skewer should come out clean, crumbs are fine! Cool on a rack and enjoy. If they are not as soft the next day you can give them a quick warm in the oven or a ping in the microwave.

# CHOCOLATE CHIP MUFFINS

## Ingredients

175g Plain Flour
45g Dark Sugar
50g Light Muscavado Sugar (Gives
a yummy caramel flavour)
1/2 tsp Baking Powder
1/2 tsp Bicarbonate of Soda
1 Lg Egg & 1 Yolk
60g Unsalted Butter
35g Veg/Sunflower oil
105g Milk
70g Yogurt
2 tsp Vanilla Extract
1/4 tsp Salt
150g Milk Choc Chips *(we recommend Callebaut)*

CALLEBAUT
BELGIUM 1911

## Method

Line your Muffin Tin with either tulip cases or muffin cases. We believe tulip cases are so much better.

Pre Heat your oven to 220C/200CFan/425F/Gas7

Into your mixing bowl add all of your dry ingredients, flour, sugars, salt and raising agents and top these with your "room temp" butter. On low and using the paddle attachment, slowly mix these together, increasing the speed, as the flour coats the butter. Once it's on a medium speed you will see what resembles breadcrumbs. Now pour in your choc chips, we do this so that they get coated with the floury, buttery mix and this will prevent them sinking into the batter. Give them a quick mix to coat them nicely.

In a separate bowl mix together all of the remaining wet ingredients, until they are all incorporated. With the paddle attachment on a low speed, pour this over the dry ingredients for no more than 15 turns of the mixer!!! Remember temperamental me!!! Once all smooth, fill each liner 3/4 full and pop into the oven for 6 mins. Then without opening the oven door reduce the temperature to 190C/170CFan/375F/Gas5 for a further 12-14 mins. Move them onto a cooling rack, once cool enough and hide them from the rest of the family!!!!

# CAKES

So let's start with the ingredients. It is worth checking the dates on your raising agents, they can go off!! And then your bake will not work as it should. To salt or not to salt, we all think it can be left out for health reasons, or maybe that's just me!! But it is an important little flavour enhancer. Salt really pulls those flavours up, so it is an essential part of the bake.

Vanilla is another important flavour enhancer, I add it everywhere!! Extract is the one you are looking for, essence is an artificial flavouring. I would always recommend a quality vanilla, unfortunately they are more expensive, but you do use less of it, so the price is really of an equal amount.

We have the cake tins we use on our Amazon Store front (see useful info) as well many other useful bits.

How do you know your cakes are cooked... every oven is different so the timings can never be 100% dead on. An oven thermometer will be your new best friend (don't go talking to it though!!!) So when your timer goes off, open the oven and using a cloth gently hit the side of the tin, does it wobble!! If it does it is not done give it longer. If there is no wobble you can now go in the the skewer. It should come out clean......crumbs are fine (I am getting a t-shirt of this!!)

Once baked remove from the oven, to aid in a flat top you can cool it upside down. If you fully lined your tin it should come off easily.

Once cool you can wrap them in cling film until needed. I have just found the amazingness that is freezing my sponges. Trim them and get them "decorate ready" before freezing. Then remove them from the freezer unwrap and decorate from frozen. The buttercream does set quicker so work a bit faster but it gives you more stability and a beautifully smooth finish. Give it a go it's amazing.

# CAKES

# OUR SIGNATURE CHOCOLATE CAKE

## Ingredients

350g Self raising Flour (If using Plain add 1 tsp of baking powder, too)
1 tsp Bicarb
Pinch of Salt
300g Caster Sugar
200g Light Brown Sugar
110g Cocoa Powder
250ml Cooled Boiled Water
100ml Vegetable Oil
100g Melted Butter
4 Large Eggs
1.5 tsp Vanilla Extract
4 tbsp Buttermilk (You can make this with 4 tbsp of milk mixed with 1/2tsp lemon juice or vinegar. Wait for 10 mins until curdled it's then ready to use)

## Method

Preheat your oven to 170C/150CFan/Gas 3/325F

Line and grease 3 x 8-inch tins.

Combine flour all the dry ingredients together, bicarb, baking powder, salt, sugars and cocoa powder using your spatula or hand whisk.

In another bowl, whisk together all of the wet ingredients, water, oil, eggs, vanilla, melted butter and buttermilk.

Then, either on low with a stand mixer or using a whisk/spatula, mix both of these until fully combined.

Do not over mix, just incorporate until it's all combined, this is a wet mix so don't worry it is right.

Pour into a jug and tip evenly into the tins.

Put it into the oven and pop your timer on for 30 to 40 minutes. (all timings vary in different ovens)

Cakes will be done when there is no wobble, and bounce back to the touch or a cocktail stick comes out clean

*Decorate with Connors Chocolate Buttercream page 150*

# DEEP CELEBRATION OMBRÉ CAKE

These beautiful soft Vanilla sponges are perfect for celebration cakes and super simple to make, the recipe creates three lovely deep six-inch cakes, each layer measuring just under three inches.

## Ingredients

180g Clover spread.
480g Plain Flour
4 tsp Baking Powder
20g Corn Flour
2 tsp Milk Powder
500g Sugar
4 large Eggs
360g Whole Milk
40g Natural Yogurt or Sour Cream
2.5 tsp Vanilla Extract
1 tsp Golden Syrup
¼ Tsp Salt

### Chocolate mix

30g Cocoa Powder
30g milk
40g warm water

1 Batch of Connors Vanilla Buttercream
1 Batch of Connors Chocolate Buttercream Pages 146/150
Chocolate Ganache to fill the layers
100g Double Cream
200g Milk Chocolate Chips

## Method

Preheat your oven to 160/140CFan/320F/Gas3
Prepare three six-inch tins, they must be at least three inches deep. If you want perfect sides, you should line them with baking paper, ideal if you are making a naked cake. I used baking belts, this not only helps the sides of the cake to bake even, but it also helps to give a moist environment to the oven. If you don't have belts, your bake may be slightly different timings, but I would pop a small tray of water in the bottom of the oven.

Mix together the chocolate mix, cocoa powder, milk and warm water in a small bowl and set aside. Beat together the clover spread and sugar until fluffy. Add in one room temperature egg at a time and mix on very low until each one is incorporated. Mix the yogurt, milk, golden syrup, vanilla, and salt together and warm to room temperature, I pop this in the microwave.
Sieve the dry ingredients together.
With the mixer on low add a third of the dry and a third of the wet, when the mixture looks uniformed after about 20 seconds scrape down (don't forget to scrape the paddle) and repeat with another third. Continue this until all is incorporated.

CALLEBAUT
BELGIUM 1911

## Method continued;

This is a wet batter, trust the process.

One final scrape down and with the mixer on medium, beat for a final 20 seconds.

This will give you 600g of batter for each tin, I find it best to weigh it in so that your cakes bake evenly.

Pour 600g of the vanilla batter into one tin, then add to the remaining mixture 2 teaspoons of the chocolate mixture you made at the start, give this a good mix and the fill the next tin with 600g of the batter.

Finally add the remaining chocolate mix to the bowl and combine, add a further 600g to the last tin (you may have a little remaining, discard this)

Pop onto the middle shelf of the oven, all three tins. Bake for 56 minutes to 1 hour. Remember all ovens are different so you should check your bake. When its springy to the touch, the sides are starting to pull away and a skewer comes out clean they are done.

Cool in the tin for 20 minutes and then release the sides gently with a knife and turn onto a cooling rack.

When almost cooled cling wrap and wait until completely chilled before cutting.

Make the Ganache by putting the cream in a bowl and popping into the microwave, bring this to a boil so that you see bubbles and steam, add in the chocolate chips and give one little stir. Set this aside for 1 minute and then stir again until it is all incorporated, cover and cool out at room temperature.

I layered my cake with chocolate buttercream forming a dam and adding in the chocolate ganache, crumb coat with the chocolate buttercream and set in the fridge until firm.

Cover with the vanilla buttercream and set again in the fridge, mix some vanilla and chocolate buttercream for the next coat, then finish with the chocolate buttercream. Setting between each coat.

Decorate the top with chocolates and candy, or make a cake pop ice cream in a waffle cone.

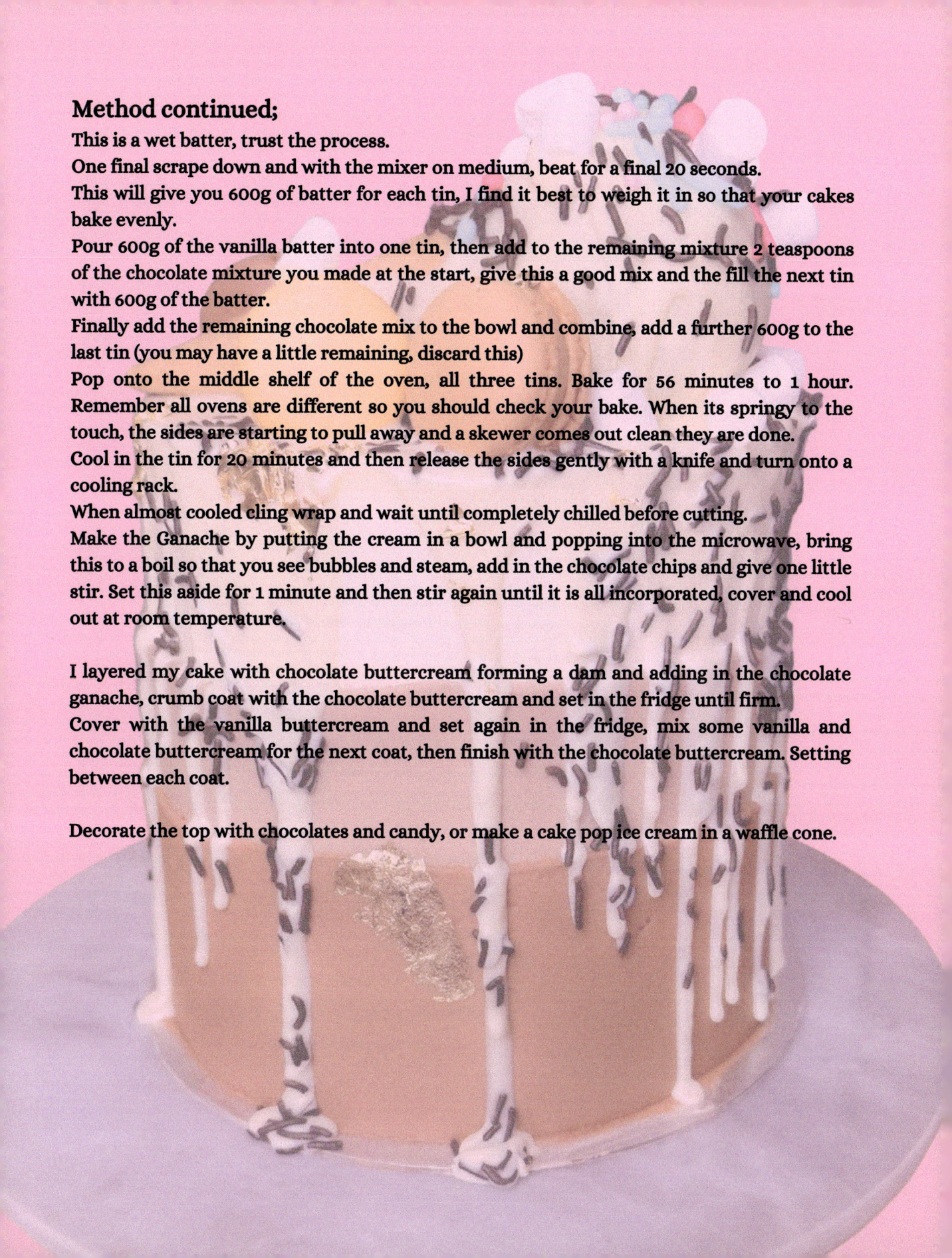

# LEMON CAKE

## Ingredients

200g Caster Sugar
185g Plain Flour
1 Tsp Baking Powder
1/4 Tsp Salt
1 Heaped Tbsp Lemon Zest
1 large Egg
66g Unsalted Butter
68g Sour Cream
70g Full Fat Plain Yogurt
2 Tsp Vanilla

## Method

This makes 1 X 6" Deep Cake. Fully line a 6"x 3" cake, tin sides too.
Pre Heat your oven to 160C/140CFan/320F/Gas3

Into your stand mixer place the flour, sugar, lemon zest, baking powder & salt. Give these a mix around and then place your "room temp" butter on the top. Using the paddle attachment on low mix these together, gradually increasing the speed to medium. You should get what will look like breadcrumbs.... I know I'm floating off to the beach with the sand again!!
In a separate bowl add the egg, sour cream, yogurt, & vanilla, mix them together and then pour slowly, over the "breadcrumby" mixture. Whip these up to a smooth batter, stopping and scraping down half way through. Don't mix too long 20 seconds, scrape, then 20 seconds should be enough.
Pour into the tin and bake for 55 mins, until a skewer comes out clean, crumbs are fine.

***Pair with either a vanilla/lemon buttercream page 146/148***

# TOFFEE APPLE CRUMBLE CAKE

## Ingredients

### Sponge

325g Plain Flour
250g Peeled & Cubed
Golden Delicious Apples
195g Golden Caster Sugar
65g Dark Brown Sugar
1 1/2 Tsp Baking Powder
130g Plain Full Fat Yogurt
52g Unsalted Melted Butter
3 Large Eggs
1/2 Tsp Salt
3 Tsp Vanilla Extract
1/2 Tbsp Milk Powder
Lemon Juice

### Crumble

200g Plain Flour
115g Unsalted butter
90g Dark Sugar

*Toffee Sauce*
*See Page 139*
*You can also use Caramel Page 138*

## Method

### Sponge

Pre Heat your oven to 170C/150Cfan/325F/Gas 3
Grease and line an 8" by 3" cake tin.

Peel, core and cube your Golden Delicious apples to around 2cm in size. Place into a bowl and squeeze over some lemon juice to prevent them going brown. Drain off any excess juice.

Place the flour, baking powder, milk powder, sugars & salt in to a bowl and fully combine. Pour the apples into this mix, this coats the apples in the flour, preventing the apples from sinking in the batter during baking.

Either by hand or on a mixer, add in the eggs, yogurt, vanilla & butter and combine. Do not over mix , as soon as the batter looks silky, pour it into your lined tin and bake for around 50-60 mins, until a skewer comes out clean.

## Crumble

200C/180CFan/400F/Gas6

Place the flour, sugar and cubed room temperature butter into the mixing bowl. With the mixer on low, using the paddle attachment combine until the ingredients resemble course breadcrumbs.

Line a flat baking tin with parchment paper and pour over the crumble mix, crumbling it up as much as possible. Place into the oven for 25 mins. Once the crumble has cooled break up any large bits and place in an air tight container until you need it.

Make the Toffee sauce and allow it to cool (make sure you cover it in cling film to prevent a skin from forming)

## Assembly

Once the cake is cold enough to use, make some holes in the top of the cake, using a skewer or something similar. This will allow the toffee/caramel sauce to fall into the cake....yummm. Pour the sauce over the cake, as much as you would like!!!

Then sprinkle over the crumble. Slice and serve.

# WHITE VELVET CAKE

## Ingredients

150g Plain Flour
160g Caster Sugar
1/8 Tsp Bicarbonate of Soda
1/4 Tsp Salt
28g Unsalted Butter
1 Egg yolk
85g Egg Whites
50g Veg/Sunflower oil
85g Buttermilk
43g Full Fat Yogurt
2 Tsp Vanilla extract
1/4 Tsp Vinegar

## Method

This makes 1 6"x 3" Deep cake. For more layers just multiply by as many as you need.

Fully line your cake tin, sides too.
Pre heat your oven to 160C/140CFan/320F/Gas3

Begin by separating your eggs (keep the remaining yolks for the other recipes that need an extra yolk, or they can be frozen)
Make sure you have cleaned the egg white bowl with lemon/vinegar, to cut through any grease.
Weigh out your sugar next and remove 2 tablespoons from it to whip up with the egg white.

Whip the egg whites in the clean bowl, when they begin foaming, slowly add in the sugar. Keep whipping until you get stiff peaks and they hold up. Pour this into a separate bowl for later.
To the sugar you weighed before, add the flour, bicarb & salt. Give them a mix up and then add your "room temp" butter to the top and mix on low, slowly increasing the speed to medium. It's ready when the mix looks like breadcrumbs/sand!!

In a separate bowl mix together the egg yolk, oil, buttermilk, yogurt, vanilla and vinegar. This can now be added to the breadcrumb mixture, whip them together until it's all incorporated and smooth. Scrape down half way through to get the bottom bits of flour.

It's now time to fold in the meringue. Take a couple of spoonfuls first and fold them in and then add the raining amount. Be sure to fold, not mix or whip, or you will loose all of that precious air. This will take a few minutes.

You can now pour the mix into the tin and bake for 55 to 60 mins

This is a beautifully soft cake, you can pair it with any of the buttercreams, but the **vanilla on page 146** would be lovely. I added **Wexford Home preserves** strawberry jam between the layers for added yumminess.

# PEANUT BUTTER & CHOCOLATE CAKE

## Ingredients

120g Plain Flour
120g Caster Sugar
80g Dark Sugar
3/4 Tsp Bicarbonate of Soda
1/8 Tsp Baking Powder
1/8 Tsp Salt
40g Melted Unsalted Butter
40g Veg/Sunflower Oil
63g Buttermilk
40g Full Fat Yogurt
35g Cooled Boiled water
1 Lg Egg
1/4 Tsp Coffee Powder
1 Tsp Vanilla Extract
44g Smooth Peanut Butter
25g Cocoa Powder

## Method

This makes 1 6"x 3" Deep cake. For more layers just multiply by as many as you need.

Fully line your cake tin, sides too.
Pre heat your oven to 160C/140CFan/320F/Gas3

You will need 2 separate bowls. In one add all of your dry ingredients, flour, sugars, raising agents and salt. Mix these well together and set to one side.

In the next bowl add in the oil, butter, peanut butter, coffee and cocoa powder. Now melt these together in the microwave. Give them a good stir after heating so that the peanut butter smooths out, if it stays clumpy just heat a little bit longer.

Now this is warm so we add the water, yogurt, buttermilk and vanilla. Stir these up and it will reduce the temperature. We can now add the egg, no one wants a scrambled egg cake!!!

Here's the simple bit, just pour the wet mix over the dry and stir them in together, you can do this by hand or in a mixer, ensure the batter is smooth though.

Tip it into the tin and bake for 55-60 mins.

Enjoy with our chocolate peanut butter, buttercream (what a mouthful!!) on *page 148*

CALLEBAUT
BELGIUM 1911

# CUBA LIBRE CAKE (RUM & COKE)

One of my favourite Cocktails with a big wedge of lime and lots of ice, made with a really good spiced rum, fantastic on holiday sitting around the pool. I don't recommended taking the cake to the pool.

## Ingredients

265g Flour
3/4 tsp Bicarbonate of soda
1/4 tsp Baking Powder
1/4 tsp Salt
200g Caster Sugar
150g Light Brown Sugar
90g Cocoa powder
60ml Spiced rum (optional, you can make this a Coke Cake, just add 60ml more Coke in)
330 ml Coke (for the cake you will only need 250 ml of the rum and coke mix so don't forget to measure out once boiled together)
75g Butter
75g Veg Oil
3 Eggs
1/2 Tbsp Vanilla Extract
45g Milk
1/2 Tsp White Wine Vinegar

## Method

Preheat the oven to 160C/140CFan/320F/Gas3

Line the bottom and sides of 3, 6 inch tins.

Put the rum and coke into a pan and bring to a boil, boil this for about 4 minutes. You are not reducing it too much but heating it together and getting rid of some of the alcohol.

Put your the flour, salt, baking powder and bicarb into a bowl and give it a good mix.

When the coke mix is ready, measure out 250ml into a bowl. Add in the butter and stir to melt, then add in the cocoa powder and oil, combine these together.
Then put the rest of the wet ingredients in and mix in and the sugars, this should now be cool enough to whisk in the eggs.

Pour this into the dry mix and give it a good whisk making sure you have no dry ingredients showing.

Pour equal amounts into your prepared tins and bake in the centre of the oven for 40 minutes, or until a skewer comes out clean.

When the cakes are cooled and levelled, if needed brush the rest of the coke mix over the top of each sponge.

I built mine with Connors Vanilla Buttercream through the middle with a generous reservoir of Lime Curd **pages 146/140**

I then covered the cake with Connors Chocolate Buttercream again the recipe is in the book. Once the buttercream was smoothed around, I used a pallet knife to take away the very top section of chocolate butter cream, and backfilled this with vanilla buttercream to resemble the top of the glass and smoothed around again. I coloured a little Vanilla buttercream with Connors Simply Colours Ivy, to a lovely lime green colour to decorate the top of the cake. I also made a fondant lime and raided my cocktail kit for some paper umbrellas, straws, and decorations. But you decorate how you like, it will be wonderful however you choose to do it.

# WHITE CHOCOLATE MUD CAKE WITH RASPBERRIES

This is a dense rich, sweet cake and extremely moorish paired with the tartness of raspberries.

## Ingredients

160g Butter
50g Vegetable Oil
320g White Chocolate
200g Caster Sugar
50g Buttermilk
190g Milk
2 Eggs
2 tsp Vanilla
330 Plain Flour
20g Corn Flour
2 1/2 tsp Baking Powder
1/4 tsp Salt
1/4 tsp Almond Essence

1 batch of Swiss Meringue
Buttercream **page 154**

CALLEBAUT
BELGIUM 1911

## Method

Preheat the oven to 170C/150CFan/325F/Gas3 Line the bottom of 3 6 inch tins and grease the sides.

Melt the butter and white chocolate together, add in the oil, sugar, buttermilk and milk. When the mixture is cool enough whisk in the vanilla, almond essence and eggs.

Pop the dry ingredients into a bowl and mix together, then add in the wet ingredients, fold together until completely combined.

Pour equal amounts of the batter into the prepared tins and bake in the centre of the oven for 50 minutes.

The tops will brown because of the white chocolate but this is normal.

Allow the cakes to cool and turn out of the tins, trim the tops and the sides if you like and sandwich together with raspberry jam and Swiss Meringue buttercream. I topped mine with freeze dried raspberries too.

# PINEAPPLE & COCONUT CAKE

This cake isn't the prettiest cake, but it is the most succulent and soft cake that tastes amazing. A family gathering will love it, proper crowd pleaser.

## Ingredients

300g Light Brown Sugar
150g Veg Oil
100g Full fat Coconut Milk
3 Large Eggs
280g Drained tinned Pineapple
110g Desiccated Coconut
1 tsp Vanilla extract
290g Plain Flour
3/4 tsp Bicarbonate of Soda
3/4 tsp Baking Powder
1/4 tsp Coconut essence or 1 tbsp Coconut liquor

150g Drained Pineapple for the middle.
Extra Coconut for decoration

1 batch of Meringue Frosting
*page 153*

## Method

Preheat the oven to 190/170CFan/375F/Gas5
Line the bottom and sides of 2 8 inch tins.

If you have pineapple rings or chunks, you will need to chop this up to a pulp, pop this in the bowl and add all the wet ingredients, including the sugar. Give this a good whisk so that the sugar and eggs have fully incorporated.

Pop in the bowl, all of the dry ingredients and fold together. Give it a good mix with a spatula until all of the ingredients are combined.

Pour equal amounts into both tins and bake in the centre of the oven for 24 to 28 minutes or until a skewer comes out clean.

To put together Chop the remaining pineapple and make our Meringue Frosting (the Recipe is in the book.).

Put one layer of the cake on your cake stand and spread the top with a generous layer of the frosting, top with the crushed pineapple and scatter in a little coconut, then add the second cake to the top. Cover all over with the meringue frosting and stipple with the back of your knife. You can scatter on more desiccated coconut at this point, leave to set up or torch with a kitchen torch for the toasted look and flavour.
It's super soft, you will need a fork to eat this cake, its not the prettiest to cut if you don't chop the pineapple finely enough too, I found that one out.

# BLACK FOREST GATEAU

A firm favourite for Christmas, this cake is so nostalgic and pairs beautifully with our stabilised whipped cream.

## Ingredients

350g Plain Flour
1 tsp Baking Powder
1 tsp Bicarbonate of Soda
1/2 tsp Salt
300g Caster Sugar
200g Light Brown Sugar
120g Cocoa Powder
175g of previously boiled water still warm with
1 tsp of Coffee Granules
75g of the liquid from the cherries
100g Melted Butter
105g Vegetable Oil
4 Large Eggs
1 tbsp Vanilla Extract
60g Milk
1/2 tsp Cider Vinegar

100g of dark chocolate in a bar.

1 Batch of our Stabilised Whipped Cream (the recipe is in the Book)
400g jar of Cherries in Kirsch (you can use canned cherries in syrup if you prefer)

## Method

Preheat the oven to 190C/170CFan/375F/Gas5 and line the bottom and sides of 3 8 inch tins.

Melt the butter and add in the cocoa powder, sugars, oil, milk & vinegar, vanilla, eggs, coffee mix and liquid from the cherries. Mix this all together ensuring that the eggs are fully beaten.

Put the remaining ingredients into a bowl and give it a stir, then add in all of the wet ingredients, give this a good mix until all is incorporated.

Bake for 28 to 30 minutes or until a skewer comes out clean.

Leave to chill in the tins for 10 minutes then turn out and cool on a rack.

To decorate make the whipped cream recipe, brush each layer of the cake with the liquid from the cherries. Pipe the cream on each layer leaving a well in the centre and smother with a healthy amount of the cherries, then grate over lots of dark chocolate, repeat this stacking the cake.

Decorate the top with the cream and cherries and another drizzle of the cherry juice. Finally a really healthy grating of the dark chocolate.

Chill the cake in the fridge until you are ready to serve.

# CHOCOLATE ORANGE CAKE

## Ingredients

125g Plain Flour
110g Caster Sugar
60g Dark Brown Sugar
1/2 Tsp Bicarbonate of Soda
1/4 Tsp Baking Powder
Zest of 3 Oranges (15g)
1/2 Tsp Salt
45g Cocoa Powder
1/4 Tsp Coffee Powder
45g Orange Juice
50g Full Fat Milk
1 Tbsp Milk Powder
75g Veg/Sunflower Oil
75g Sour Cream
1 Lg Egg
1 1/2 Tsp Vanilla

## Method

This makes 1 6"x 3" Deep cake. For more layers just multiply by as many as you need.

Fully line your cake tin, sides too.
Pre heat your oven to 160C/140CFan/320F/Gas3

Place all of your dry ingredients into a bowl, flour, sugars, raising agents, salt and orange zest. Give these a good mix together.

In another bowl add in your milk, orange juice, cocoa powder, coffee and milk powder. Heat these in the microwave to pull out the flavour of the cocoa powder and activate the milk powder. Now this is hot so to cool the mix we add in the oil, sour cream, and vanilla. Mix these together and now you can add in the egg, give it a final stir.

Pour this over the dry ingredients and either by hand or in the mixer whip them all together until the batter is all smooth. Don't over mix 1 minute is enough.

The smell of the orange should be amazing.... Oh yeah!!!!
Pour into the tin and bake for 55-60 mins, until a skewer comes out clean, crumbs are fine.

Pair this with either a chocolate buttercream or our chocolate orange buttercream **pages 148/150**

# COFFEE & WALNUT CAKE

## Ingredients

180g Plain Flour
90g Dark Brown Sugar
95g Golden Caster Sugar
1/4 Tsp Bicarbonate of Soda
1/2 Tsp Salt
40g Unsalted Butter
50g Chopped Walnuts (around 2cm big)
1/4 Tsp Cinnamon
1 - 1 1/2 Tbsp Coffee Powder depending on taste**
100g Full Fat Milk
70g Veg/Sunflower Oil
50g Sour Cream
2 Tsp Vanilla Extract
1/2 Tsp White Wine/Cider Vinegar
100g Egg White
1 Egg Yolk

## Method

This makes 1 6"x 3" Deep cake. For more layers just multiply by as many as you need.

Fully line your cake tin, sides too.
Pre heat your oven to 160C/140CFan/320F/Gas3

Begin by separating your eggs, make sure you clean out your egg white bowl with lemon juice or vinegar, to cut through any grease. We have other recipes where you can use the spare egg yolks or you can freeze them.

Weigh out your sugars and then remove 2 tablespoons from it, to stabilise the egg whites. Begin whipping your egg whites and when it becomes foamy, sprinkle the sugar in slowly whilst the mixer is still going. The sugar will help to stiffen the egg white, they will be done when they hold their own form, or you can turn it upside down and not decorate your floor!!!! Set this to one side.

To the remaining sugars now add the flour, raising agents, cinnamon and salt, give these a mix together. Now place the "room Temp" butter on the top and mix on low, building up steadily, with the paddle attachment, until it resembles sand! I like sand so I'm sticking with that!!! To this sprinkle on the walnuts and whip them in, this will coat them, preventing them from sinking in the batter.

In a separate bowl add the coffee powder and full fat milk together, heat these in the microwave to pull out the coffee flavour. Now this is hot , so we need to cool it down, add the oil, sour cream, vanilla and vinegar to the mix and give it a good stir. Now it has cooled add in the egg yolk and pour this mix over the sandy mixture. Give this a good whip scraping down half way through, pulling the flour off the bottom of the bowl. Don't over whip the mix a minute is plenty.

Ok time to fold in the egg white. Begin by taking a few spoonfuls and initially folding this in. Then you can pour in the rest, ensure you are folding, not stirring or whipping. this is the only way to protect all that air you worked so hard for!!(well the mixer did but hey we need some praise). This will take a few mins. When you can't see those lumps of meringue anymore, it is time to pour the mix into the tin and bake.

This will take 55-60 minutes in the oven and when the skewer comes out clean, it's all cooked. Crumbs are fine... it feels like this is my new slogan!!! Could I make a song out of it!!

*Pair this with a beautiful Coffee Buttercream or Vanilla Pages 146/148*

**Ok let's talk Coffee, so the general rule is if you wouldn't drink it, don't use it in the cake. I like to use a fine coffee powder, I find that they are smoother giving a much more luxurious flavour. You can also use espresso just remove the liquid content from the milk.

# MADERIA POUND CAKE

Madeira cake was a childhood favourite for me with lots of custard, as an adult I use Madeira wine lots in cooking. It's fortified like a sherry so tastes delicious. Imagine my surprise when I started to research Madeira cakes as I wanted to make one, What No Madeira in there???? So I decided to make this right. Here is our version, not technically correct but beautiful nonetheless.

## Ingredients

180g Soft Butter
340g Caster Sugar
345g Plain Flour
1 Tbsp Baking Powder
1/2 tsp Salt

4 Eggs
150g Yogurt
45g Milk
1 1/2 tbsp of Madeira wine
1 tbsp of Vanilla extract

200g Icing Sugar
35g Water or milk (or go rouge and use a little more Madeira)

*Blueberry Jam Page 141*

## Method

Preheat the oven to 170C/150CFan/325F/Gas3
Grease a bunt tin and dust with flour, you will see if you have missed any areas by the flour. If you have go back in, you don't want to loose half of your cake.

Cream the butter and sugar together until light and fluffy, add in the eggs one at a time and cream in on a low speed.
Warm the vanilla, Madeira, milk and yogurt a little in the microwave to get to room temperature.
Add in the dry ingredients and start to mix on low as it starts to form a paste slowly pour in the wet ingredients stopping half way and scraping down the bowl, add the rest of the wet slowly and beat on medium for 30 seconds until you have a smooth batter.

Pour into your greased and floured bunt tin and bake for 50 minutes or until a skewer comes out clean.

Rest in the tin for half an hour, then turn the tin over onto a cooling rack, don't touch the tin, just allow gravity to do its thing, 30 seconds to a minute and it will slide nicely down in one piece.
When it is completely cool, mix your icing with the liquid of your choice and drizzle over the top, then spoon on some blueberry jam. (See our Blueberry Jam recipe in the book)

Slice up and enjoy, especially good with Custard.

# GLUTEN & DAIRY FREE VANILLA SPONGE

## Ingredients

360g Vegetable Oil
9 large Eggs
3/4 tsp Xantham Gum (if your rice flour already contains Xantham Gum omit this)
3 tsp Baking Powder
465g Doves Plain Flour
570g Icing Sugar (it is important to use icing sugar to ensure an emulsified mix)
1/2 tsp Salt
3 tsp Vanilla Extract

## Method

Oven Temp 180C/160CFab/350F/Gas4
In a stand mixer fitted with the whisk attachment, whisk together the eggs and oil until combined and a little frothy. This will take a few minutes.
Sieve together all of your dry ingredients and mix to combine.
Add the dry into the wet mix along with the vanilla.
Whisk on low to gently combine, you will see little lumps in the batter. Once combined turn the mixer to high, no need to worry about over mixing as you have no gluten to battle. Mix for a few minutes and scrape down, mix again on high until you have a mix that looks like a soft whipped cream, hols a few ribbons on the surface and has no lumps, about 2 1/2 minutes on high.
Transfer to your lined tins, around 465g of mix per pan, and bake for 30 to 32 minutes.
Leave to cool in the tins for 10 minutes before turning out.
To make this into cupcakes, this mix will make 24, around 75g to 80g of batter per case. Bake for 22 minutes on 160 fan.
If you half the mix, you must half an egg to ensure you get 4 1/2 eggs.

# PEANUT BUTTER & JAM CAKE

## Ingredients

160g Plain Flour
100g Caster Sugar
100 Light Brown Sugar
1 Tsp Baking Powder
1/2 Tsp Salt
1 Lg egg
45g Unsalted Butter
70g Full Fat Yogurt
25g Full Fat Milk
45g Smooth Peanut Butter
35g Strawberry Stuff *Page 142*
2 Tsp Vanilla Extract

## Method

This makes 1 6"x 3" Deep cake. For more layers just multiply by as many as you need.

Fully line your cake tin, sides too.
Pre heat your oven to 160C/140CFan/320F/Gas3

Into your mixer bowl add in your flour, sugars, baking powder and salt. Mix these together, then add your "room temp" butter and turn the mixer on low. Once the flour begins to be coated in the butter turn the speed up to medium until you get a soft breadcrumb texture.

In a separate bowl, mix together, your egg, yogurt, milk, strawberry stuff, peanut butter and vanilla. Pour this slowly over your breadcrumb mixture whilst the speed is on low. Do not over mix 20-30 seconds then scrape down and repeat for another 20 seconds until the batter is all smooth and combined. Pop this into your tin and bake for 55 to 60 mins.

Pair this with our peanut butter, buttercream **page 148** and use a lovely layer of strawberry jam between the layers, I use *Wexford Home Preserves*

Wexford Home Preserves

# "MOCHA" CHOCOLATE & COFFEE CAKE

## Ingredients

120 Plain Flour
1/4 Tsp Baking Powder
1/2 Tsp Bicarbonate of Soda
100g Golden Caster Sugar
80g Dark brown Sugar
45g Cocoa Powder
1 Tbsp Milk Powder
1 Tbsp Coffee Powder
1/2 Tsp Salt
45g Cooled Boiled Water
75g Veg/Sunflower Oil
50g Full Fat Yogurt
75g Full Fat Milk
1 Lg Egg
1 Tsp Vanilla Extract

### Simple Syrup

50g Dark Brown Sugar
50g Water
2 Tsp Coffee Powder
1 Tsp Vanilla

Ok let's talk Coffee, so the general rule is if you wouldn't drink it, don't use it in the cake. I like to use a fine coffee powder, I find that they are smoother giving a much more luxurious flavour. You can also use espresso just remove the liquid content from the milk.

## Method

This makes 1 6"x 3" Deep cake. For more layers just multiply by as many as you need.

Fully line your cake tin, sides too.
Pre heat your oven to 160C/140CFan/320F/Gas3

Into a bowl place all of your dry ingredients, flour, raising agents, sugars and salt. Mix these together well and leave to one side for later.

Grab a second bowl, place in your water, milk, cocoa powder, coffee and milk powder, heat these in the microwave, we are doing this to bring out the flavours and activate the milk powder.
This is now a bit hot, so to cool it add in the yogurt, oil and vanilla, mix it around and it will now be cool enough to add the egg. Stir these together and then pour it over the dry ingredients. Mix either by hand or mixer, but make sure the batter is all smooth and silky. Try not to over mix a minute should be plenty.

Pop into the oven and bake for 55 to 60 mins, A skewer should come out clean, crumbs are fine!! (Oh I'm singing this now!!)

When the cakes are baked and cool enough to touch, poke random holes into the top of the sponge, with a skewer or something similar.

Let's make the syrup. In a saucepan pour in the sugar, water and coffee and bring this to the boil. Let it simmer for 2 mins and then remove it from the heat. Tip in the vanilla and stir it in. Grab a dessert/soup spoon and drizzle around 4-5 spoonfuls of the mix over the top of the sponge, whilst the syrup and cake are still warm. The syrup will soak through the sponge enhancing the flavour.

**You can decorate this with our mocha or chocolate buttercream page 155/150**

*I added some caramel  between the layers for a Caramel Mocha Flavour*

# CARAMEL CAKE

## Ingredients

80g Golden Caster Sugar
100g Light Brown Sugar
20g Dark Brown Sugar
185g Plain Flour
1/8 Tsp Bicarbonate of Soda
1/4 Tsp Baking Powder
1/2 Tsp Salt
1 Lg Egg
65g Unsalted Butter
70g Sour Cream
70g Full Fat Milk
2 Tsp Vanilla Extract

## Method

This makes 1 6"x 3" Deep cake. For more layers just multiply by as many as you need.

Fully line your cake tin, sides too.
Pre heat your oven to 160C/140CFan/320F/Gas3

Into your mixer place the flour, sugars, raising agents and salt. Give them a mix together, and then add your "room temp" butter. Begin mixing these on a low speed and gradually move up to medium. When it looks like soft breadcrumbs turn off the mixer and move onto the wet ingredients.

In a separate bowl mix together the egg, sour cream, milk and vanilla. With the mixer on low, pour this over the breadcrumb mixture slowly. Whip it up for around 20-30 seconds, scrape down and then give it a final mix for 20 seconds. The batter should be all smooth. Pour this into the cake tin and bake for 55 to 60 mins.

I pair this with the salted caramel buttercream **page 148**

Traybakes & Bars

# CORNFLAKE CRUNCH BAR

## Ingredients

500g Callebaut Milk Chocolate 823 ( we recommend Callebaut but you can substitute )
100g Rice Krispies
200g Corn Flakes
250g Golden Syrup
** for additional flavours try adding
Marshmallows
Coconut
An additional layer of caramel between the chocolate and cornflakes
1/4 tsp Almond Essence into warmed golden syrup. (Warming will allow the essence to mix well)

## Method

Begin by lining a 7 x 11" Cake tin. I prefer to line the bottom and the sides, for a clean look around the sides.
Melt your chocolate in the microwave
* If you are using Callebaut, keep the temperature under 30C/85F at all times and the chocolate will remain in temper and have a perfect structure, giving a great snap.
Add your Rice Krispies to the melted chocolate, give it a good stir and pour into the lined tin. Pop this into the fridge.......go on eat the bits left on the spoon its rude not too!!!!!
Move onto the Corn Flakes once the choc/krispy bottom has set.
Measure out the Corn Flakes and drizzle over the golden syrup. This is sticky business so I use gloves and get my hands in there.. it's easier!!
Pour over the chocky base and using a potato masher push it all down to fill the gaps. Don't push too hard or they will all break up, you still want that Corn Flake look.
Melt some more chocolate and using a piping bag drizzle across the top.
Pop it back into the fridge to set then cut it up and enjoy
Yummmmm xxxxxxx

# STRAWBERRY & WHITE CHOCOLATE CRUNCH BAR

### Ingredients

### Base

100g Oats ( Gluten Free Oats)

200g Unsalted Butter

200g Plain Flour ( Doves Gluten Free Plain Flour)

100g Golden Caster Sugar

2 Large Egg Yolks

2 tsp Milk Powder

1 tsp Vanilla Extract

Pinch of Salt

120g White Chocolate Chips ( We use Callebaut W2 White chocolate Callets )

### Filling

You can use Shop bought Strawberry Jam or make your own. Here in Ireland I use
***Wexford Home Preserves*** as *"every product is handmade in small batches using
the traditional open pot boiling method. The best quality ingredients are sourced
as locally as possible and all preserves are 100% natural"*

I used 600g of Jam

### Crumble

100g Oats ( Gluten Free Oats)

100g Plain Flour ( Doves Plain Gluten Free )

100g Salted Butter

100g Golden Caster Sugar

1 tbsp Golden Syrup

# Method

## Cookie Base

Line a 8" X 8" tin. (mine is around 1 inch deep)

Pre-Heat the oven to 180C/160CFan/350F/Gas 4

Melt your butter in the microwave, and place on the side to cool.

Pour the oats, flour, salt, sugar & milk powder into a bowl and mix them together so that they are fully incorporated.

To this, pour over the COOLED melted butter and stir in gently, until just incorporated.

Add the 2 egg yolks and the white chocolate chips, give the mix a final stir and pour into the lined tin.

Level off and stab the mix with a fork, this will stop the mix rising and getting air bubbles. Do this all over the cookie dough.

Bake in the oven for 25-27 mins. You want it to look brown around the edges.

## Crumble

Pour the oats, flour & sugar into a bowl and mix thoroughly. To this pour over the melted salted butter and golden syrup. ( *If you don't want it too sweet you can leave this out but I love it!!)

Mix all of this together, I pop on a pair of gloves and get my hands in there, it comes together so much better. Leave this on the side to rest.

## Filling

Once the cookie base is out of the oven allow it to cool, for around 10 mins, in the tin, on a cooling rack.

Pour the Jam over the base and smooth it out.

Sprinkle the crumble mix over the top, so that it fully covers the Jam, place this back into the oven (at the same temperature as the base) for 30 minutes.

The crumble should have turned a lovely sandy colour and have bubbling Jam oozing around the edges.

Allow this to cool, in the tin until it is at a safe temperature to place into the fridge. I keep mine in for around an hour and then use a knife to loosen the sticky Jam away from the sides, then remove the "crumble crunch" from the tin, slice up and enjoy.

Serve either hot or cold, with a lovely blob of cream, ice cream or custard.

# PECAN & WHITE CHOCOLATE BLONDIE

## Ingredients

335g Unsalted Butter
150g Light Brown Sugar
150g Dark Brown Sugar
3 Large Eggs
250g Plain Flour
Pinch of Salt
2 Tsp Vanilla Extract
2 Tsp Milk Powder
350g White Chocolate we use Callebaut W2
200g Pecans ( chopped into quarters )

## Method

Fully Line (sides too) a 7" X 11" Cake Tin approx 3 inch deep.

Pre heat your oven to 200C/180CFan/390F/Gas6

In a bowl add all of your dry ingredients in together flour, milk powder, salt, chocolate chips & pecans. Mix all of these fully together.
Pop your butter and sugars into a microwavable bowl and heat these together, until the temperature reaches around 60C, let this fully cool before adding it to any other ingredients.
In a separate bowl add the eggs and vanilla together and pour over the dry ingredients.
Now cool add in the butter/sugar mix and stir the batter all together.
Pour into the tin.
Bake for 35 to 40 mins. There should be a slight give on the top but not a wobble of jelly. Let's aim for a set custard consistency.
Now for the hard bit....... Let it cool fully (2 hours!!) then if you want perfectly cut pieces, it needs to go into the fridge for another 2 hours!!!
Now remove from the tin slice up and enjoy.

CALLEBAUT®
BELGIUM 1911

# PISTACHIO & RASPBERRY BLONDIE

## Ingredients

### Blondie
100g Melted Unsalted Butter
125g White Chocolate melted we use Callebaut
40g Caster Sugar
40g Soft Brown Brown Sugar
2 Large Eggs
1 tsp Milk Powder
110g Plain Flour
1/2 tsp Baking Powder
1 tsp Vanilla Extract
1/4 tsp Salt
70g White chocolate Chips
80g Crushed Pistachios

### Raspberry Jam
120g Frozen Raspberries
60g Sugar
2 tbs Water
1/4 tsp salt

# Method

## To make the Jam.

Place all the ingredients in a saucepan, bring to a boil and crush with a potato masher, turn the heat to a simmer and keep going for about 10 minutes or until when you pop the sauce on a plate to cool it has a slight set. Push through a metal sieve to remove seeds and set aside to cool slightly.

## For the Blondie.

Pre heat the oven to 160 C Fan, line a baking tray, base and sides, I have used a 7inch by 10inch tray.

Melt the chocolate and butter together taking care not to overheat, mix in the sugar and allow to cool a little before adding the eggs. Whisk in the eggs, vanilla, salt and milk powder.

Add in most of the chopped pistachios and white chocolate chips, holding a few of each back to decorate the top, fold them through and then add in the flour and baking powder, fold gently and stop when you can't see any dry mix.

Transfer to the prepared baking tray spreading out evenly.

Spoon on the Raspberry jam in little dollops evenly and then run a knife through to marble it slightly.

Add the rest of the pistachios and white chocolate to the top and bake in the centre of the oven for 28 to 35 minutes.

Allow to cool completely in the baking tray and chill in the fridge before removing and cutting.

# CARAMEL & CINNAMON TRAYBAKE

## Ingredients

100g Melted Butter
150g Caramel (tinned or homemade)
50g Light Brown Sugar
50g Caster Sugar
2 Eggs
1/2 tsp Cinnamon
1/4 tsp salt
1 tsp Vanilla extract
60g Whole Milk
150g Plain Flour
10g Corn Flour
15g Milk Powder
1 tsp baking powder

## Toppings

200g Milk Chocolate
100g White Chocolate
150g Double Cream
50g caramel
Caramel Fudge or caramel chunks

## Method

Preheat the oven to 180C/160CFan/350F/Gas4

Line a 12 by 8 inch tray.

Melt the butter and caramel together in a pan, add in the sugars, cold milk and vanilla.

When the mixture is cool enough, beat in the eggs and cinnamon.

Mix all the dry ingredients together and add into the mixture, fold this in and mix until you see no dry mix.

Pour into the lined tray and spread out evenly. Bake for 18 minutes.

Cool in the tray on a cooling rack.

Heat your cream to 70 degrees centigrade and pour 100g into the milk chocolate and 50g into the white chocolate stir them both until they are completely melted.

Spread the milk chocolate ganache over the cooled sponge and pipe or drizzle the white and caramel over the top and decorate with the fudge pieces.

Allow the ganache to set up and slice into desired pieces.

# BROWNIE, COOKIE DOUGH CHEESECAKE BAR

## Ingredients

### Cookie Dough

150g Melted Butter
75g Caster Sugar
75g Light Brown Sugar
1 Large egg
1 tsp Vanilla Extract
260g Plain Flour
20g Corn Flour
1/2 tsp Baking Powder
1/2 tsp Bicarbonate of Soda
1/4 tsp Salt
100g White Chocolate Chips
100g Milk Chocolate Chips
We recommend Callebaut

### Cheesecake

35g Natural full fat Yogurt
350g Full Fat Cream Cheese
1/2 tbsp Vanilla Extract
125g Caster Sugar
2 Large Eggs
1 tsp Corn flour

### Brownie

120g Melted Butter
140g Dark Chocolate Melted
210g Caster Sugar
2 Large Eggs
1 tsp Milk Powder
30g Cocoa Powder
85g Plain Flour
1/2 tsp Baking Powder
1 tsp Vanilla Extract
75g Milk or Dark Chocolate Chips

# Method

Fully Line a 10 x 10 inch square tin, ensure that the paper overlaps the top of the tin so you can use this to remove the bake. This is best done with 2 sheets that overlay each other.

To make the cookie dough, add the sugars to the melted butter and mix together, beat in the egg and vanilla until it is a smooth mix.

Add in the dry ingredients and mix by hand until almost incorporated, then add in the chocolate chips and finish mixing, stop as soon as you all the flour is incorporated and the chocolate is evenly distributed.

Press the cookie dough into an even layer in the base of your lined tin and smooth with an offset pallet knife, if your tin will fit in the freezer place in there and freeze until solid, if not pop it in the fridge for 1 hour until you can removed it in one whole slab from the tin, then wrap and freeze until solid.
Once frozen put the cookie slab to one side if it was frozen in the tin keeping it frozen until you are ready for it.

Place the Baking paper back in the tin, so that it is fully lined again.

When the cookie dough is ready pre heat the oven to 160 fan.

Make the brownie batter by mixing the melted butter and chocolate together, then beat in the sugar, vanilla and eggs (only add the eggs if the mix is not too hot.
Add in all of the dry ingredients and Chocolate chips, fold into the mixture taking care not to over-mix.
Spread this into the base of the lined tin.

Make the cheesecake mixture by adding the yogurt, cream cheese and vanilla into a bowl and whisking together, add the eggs and whisk again until they are incorporated.

Pop the sugar and corn flour into the bowl and mix in until it is smooth.

Remove the frozen cookie dough slab from the freezer and carefully put this back into the tin on top of the brownie mixture, ensuring that it is flat to the mix.

Pour the Cheesecake mixture over the cookie slab.

Gently transfer the tin to the oven on the middle shel and bake for 45 to 50 minutes. You should have a set centre but still have a slight wobble.

Allow to cool and then refrigerate, preferably overnight. Lift from the tin using the baking paper and slice with a clean hot knife for perfect slices.

# CRACKLE TOP FUDGY BROWNIE

## Ingredients

150g Plain Flour
300g Unsalted Butter
100g Light Brown Sugar
200g Dark Brown Sugar
50g Caster Sugar
4 Large Eggs
70g Cocoa Powder ( we use Callebaut Plein Arome
2 Tsp Milk Powder
1 Tsp Coffee, Mixed with 1 Tbsp Water
Pinch Salt
300g Chocolate Chips of your choice we use Callebaut Callets

## Method

Fully Line a 7" x 11' Cake Tin (mine is around 2' deep)

Pre Heat your oven to 190C/170CFan/375f/Gas5

Into a microwaveable bowl, add your cubed butter, sugars, milk powder, salt, coffee and cocoa powder together and microwave these, take the temperature to around 60C. The heat will help with the crackle top, intensify the cocoa powder and just make all the flavours yummier!!!!

Now put this to one side to cool, or you are going to end up with scrambled eggs.

In a separate bowl add in your flour and chocolate chips, give these a mix up.

Once your warm mix has cooled enough to below 20C add in your eggs and mix up, pour this over the flour and the chips. Give these a good mix until you get a lovely smooth batter.

Pour into your tin and bake in the oven for 20-25 mins. You are looking for the mix to have a feel of set custard, not be set like a cake or be too loose like jelly.

Allow the brownie to cool for at least an hour, I recommend popping it into the fridge after this time (ensure it is cool), it will slice so much better. For selling purposes, to get that clean edge leave it in the fridge until the next day, or for at least 8 hours. You will get a perfect slice then.

You can also fill this with any goodies you like, Crunchie, Kinder, Chomp Pieces.......ohhhh yummmmmm....

CALLEBAUT®
BELGIUM 1911

# COCONUT BROWNIE BAR

## Ingredients

### Brownie

160g Plain Flour
200g Dark Brown Sugar
200g Golden Caster Sugar
150g Desiccated Coconut
1 Tsp Coffee Powder
1/8 Tsp Salt
70g Cocoa Powder
280g Unsalted Butter
5 Large Eggs

### Ganache

500g Milk/Plain Chocolate ( We
recommend Callebaut 823/811)
250g Double/Heavy Cream

CALLEBAUT®
BELGIUM 1911

## Method

Fully Line a 7" x 11' Cake Tin (mine is around 2'
deep)

Pre Heat your oven to 190C/170CFan/375f/Gas5

In a bowl place your butter, coffee, cocoa
powder & sugars. Melt all of these in the
microwave to around 50C. Now add in your
coconut and stir it all around. Once the batter
has come to around 20-25C add in your eggs
and again stir them in to create a silky batter.
(You can use the mixer). Finally add the flour
and salt and again mix together.

Pour into your your tin and bake for around 35
mins. You are looking for the consistency to be
like set custard when you "knock" the tin.
Allow the brownie to cool for at least an hour, I
recommend popping it into the fridge after this
time (ensure it is cool), it will slice so much
better. To make the ganache, place your
chocolate and cream into a bowl and
microwave it until it is all melted. Remove it
before you think it is done, or you may scold
the chocolate. Keep stirring until the ganache is
lovely and silky (melt for short bursts if the
ganache is not properly melted). Pour this over
the brownie and allow the chocolate to set.
 For selling purposes, to get that clean edge
leave it in the fridge until the next day, or for at
least 8 hours. You will get a perfect slice then.

# SPICED CARROT CAKE TRAYBAKE

## Ingredients

200g Soft Brown Sugar
180g Sunflower Oil
2 Large Eggs
185g Finley grated Carrots
75g Chopped Pecan Nuts
1/2 tsp Ground Ginger
1/2 tsp Ground Cinnamon
1/4 tsp Ground Allspice
1/4 tsp orange oil or the zest of one orange
1/2 tsp of Vanilla Extract
190g Plain Flour
1/2 tsp Bicarbonate of Soda
1/2 tsp Baking powder

310g Icing Sugar
1/4 tsp salt
50g Soft Butter
1/2 tsp Vanilla Extract
120g Cream Cheese

## Method

Preheat the oven to 180C/160CFan/350F/Gas4
Line a 6 1/2 x 10 inch brownie sheet.

In a large bowl, whisk together the sugar, oil and eggs. Add in the carrots, nuts, spices and flavourings and mix together. Put the dry ingredients into bowl and mix together, then add these to the wet and fold in until you have no dry mix.
Pour the mix into the baking sheet and level out.
Bake in the centre of the oven for 30 to 33 minutes or until a skewer comes out clean.

Cool in the tin.

To make the cream cheese frosting, sift the icing sugar into the bowl of a stand mixer with the paddle attachment on, add in the soft butter. On low, mix this until you have a light breadcrumb texture, clean down the paddle and bowl to ensure there is no butter left.

Add in the cream cheese, salt and vanilla and mix on low until almost incorporated and scrape down. Turn the mixer to medium and beat until smooth.

When the Carrot Cake is cool, use an offset spatula to roughly cover the the top with the frosting.

Add on Carrot shaped decorations and chill in the fridge for an hour until the topping is set.

Slice into 12 pieces with a clean warm knife.

# SUPER SOFT WHITE VELVET TRAYBAKE

## Ingredients

300g Plain Flour
315g Caster Sugar
1/4 Tsp Bicarbonate of Soda
1/2 Tsp Salt
55g Unsalted Butter
170g Egg White
170g Buttermilk
85g Full Fat Yogurt
160g Veg/Sunflower Oil
3 Tsp Vanilla Extract
1/2 Tsp White Wine/Cider Vinegar

## Method

Fully line a 7" x 11' Tin, sides too. My tin is 2" in depth

Pre Heat your oven to Pre heat your oven to 160C/140CFan/320F/Gas3

Begin by separating your eggs, before placing your egg whites into a bowl, ensure you have cleaned it with lemon juice or vinegar, this will cut through any grease. (We have other recipes that need egg yolk, so no need to waste them, or they can be frozen). Leave the whites separate and set to one side.

Weigh out your sugar and remove 2 tablespoon from this, we need to use this to stabilise the eggs when we whip them.

In the clean bowl, whip up the egg whites, building up the speed gently, once it has become fuller and foamy, slowly add the sugar whilst whipping. The meringue is done when it looks all silky and holds its own form. Tip it upside down, go on... is it still in the bowl? If so it's all ready, if it fell out I am so sorry, it was not quite stiff enough!!!!! Leave this to one side.

To the weighed out sugar now add in the flour, raising agents and salt. Place these together in the mixer with the paddle attachment on. Give them a mix and once it's all combined place the "room temperature" butter on the top and with the mixer on low to begin with, whip these up. Gradually increase the speed to medium and once it resembles... you know it breadcrumbs/sand, it's all done.

Grab another bowl and to this add the buttermilk, yogurt, oil, vanilla and vinegar. Mix these together, then pour over the breadcrumb mix. Whip for around 20 seconds on medium, scrape down, making sure to get the flour at the bottom. Then mix again for another 20 seconds.

It's now time to fold in the egg whites. Initially just add a few spoonfuls and fold these in. You must fold gently, not whip or mix, that will knock out all of the precious air. Now pour in the rest of the egg white and fold it all in. This will take a few mins, but so worth it. When you can no longer see little egg white cloudy blobs it's all ready. Pour into your time and bake for an hour.

This is so soft so try not to mess with it until it is cool. Top this with a Vanilla Buttercream on **page 146**

*This is too soft to use as a cake, the bottom layer would be just like a sponge and bow under the weight.

# RED VELVET TRAYBAKE

## Ingredients

70g Soft Butter
10g Cocoa Powder
155g Plain Flour
1/4 tsp Salt
1/2 tsp Bicarbonate of Soda
140g Caster Sugar
1/2 tsp Red Food Colouring (I used Poppy extra from Connors Simply Colours Range)
1 tsp Vanilla Extract
140g Buttermilk
1 Large Egg
1 tsp white wine vinegar

## Method

Preheat the oven to 155 C Fan.

Line a 12 by 7 inch baking tray or disposable foil tray.

Take 40g of buttermilk from the ingredients and add the 1/2 tsp of food colouring into the milk, give this a whisk to fully incorporate and then add in the rest of the buttermilk and warm in the microwave for 30 to 45 seconds, you want it to be about 35 degrees C.

Put all the dry ingredients including the sugar into the bowl of the mixer with the paddle attachment on, add in the butter and mix until you have a crumble like consistency.

To the warmed buttermilk add the vanilla, egg and vinegar and whisk to combine.

With the mixer on low, slowly pour in the wet mix a little at a time, stop half way and scrape down then finish adding the wet. Mix on medium for 30 seconds until you have a nice even batter.
Pour this into your tray, if you are using a disposable tray, place it on a solid tray first to avoid spilling the mix.

Bake in the centre of the oven for 20 to 22 minutes.

When cooled decorate with our cream cheese frosting, ***page 145***

# Baking It Simple

## WITH JINNY & JO

# CHOCOLATE LOAF CAKE

## Ingredients

50g melted butter
30g melted milk chocolate
125g cooled boiled water
20g vegetable oil
55g sour Cream
2 eggs
1 tsp vanilla extract
1/2 tablespoon golden syrup
150g caster sugar
100g light brown sugar
175g plain flour
1 tsp baking powder
1/2 tsp bicarbonate of soda
Pinch of salt
55g cocoa powder
1 tsp instant coffee
1 tsp milk powder

## Method

Pre heat the oven to 155 C Fan.

Add all the dry ingredients into a bowl and mix together.

Melt the butter and chocolate together until just melted and add in all the wet ingredients, then add in the sugars to combine. If the mix is cool enough add in the eggs and give it a good whisk.

Mix the wet into the dry and pour into a lined loaf tin.

Bake for 1hr to 1hr 10 minutes or until a skewer comes out clean.

Once cooled, Turn out and slice into 3 Layers.

Fill with the buttercream and flavour of your choice. I used Swiss meringue Buttercream, Caramel and crushed Maltesers.

# Cookies

# &

# Biscuits

# DEEP DISH COOKIE PIE

## Ingredients

### Cookie Dough

210g Unsalted Room Temp Butter (see below video for help)
300g Plain Flour
83g Caster Sugar
83g Light Brown Sugar
1 & 1/2 Tbsp Golden Syrup
1 Large Egg & 1 Egg Yolk
3/4 Tsp Baking Powder
1/2 Tsp Bicarbonate of Soda
1 & 1/2 Tsp Vanilla Extract
1/8 Tsp Almond Essence
225g Slightly Crushed Chocolate of your choice Maltesers/Crunchie/Mini Eggs Etc.
105g White Chocolate Chips (we recommend Callebaut )

### For the Filling

Any other mini choc of your choice....
mini mars, or more broken up chocolate bars yummmm!!!

### For the Ganache

400g Milk Chocolate
150g Double Cream

## Method

Pre Heat the oven to 200C/180Cfan/390F/Gas 6
I recommend NOT using the Fan setting, give it a try without!!!

Using our room temp butter (PAGE...) add it to the mixer along with the sugars and golden syrup. Mix on medium until fluffy and lighter in colour.

Scrape down

Now add in ALL of the other ingredients and mix on low until it is just incorporated, try not to overmix.

Bring the mixture together and remove from the bowl.

You should have around 1050g of Cookie Dough.

Use an 8 Inch tin with 1 & 1/2 inch depth ( line it if not using silicone like I do). Then separate the dough into 2 batches. Approx 360g for the top and 690g for the bottom and sides. Place the top part into a ziploc bag and place into the fridge.

Now cover the bottom and sides of the tin around 1 to 1 & 1/2cm thickness. Take off pieces and kind of stick it all together in the tin.

Once covered and all sealed place the tin into the freezer for 30 mins.

Whist you wait we can make the ganache.

Pour the cream over the chocolate and melt in 30 second bursts, stirring well in between. Try not to over heat the chocolate, heating it upto 38C will be fine.

Cover the ganache in cling film touching the top and wait for it to cool. Now we will make the lid.

# Method Continued

Take the cookie pie top from the fridge and using a piece of parchment paper, use your hands to push the dough flat until it becomes just a few cm larger than the tin. I don't use a rolling pin as cookie batter can be hard to roll and will break up. Be very careful to have no tears or holes as the filling will leak through, again it needs to be around 1 & 1/2 cm thick. now place the dough on something flat, so it doesn't lose shape and place into the freezer.

Remove the pie from the freezer and pour in enough ganache, to fill just slightly under half way up the pie. Now add in the broken up chocolate of your choice. Do not push them down, just let them sit there)

Pour on the remaining ganache leaving a 1 cm gap from the top. You don't want the filling to be able to ooze out when baking. Top with more chockies of your choice, Back into the freezer for a further 10 mins.

SOOOOOOO nearly there, remove from the freezer again, along with the top. Turn the top upside down onto the cookie pie with the paper still attached for stability. Push the top down gently and then peel off the paper. Seal the top around the edges so that the filling can't ooze out , don't let it hang over as it will pull the lid down with cooking and tear the top, then…….sorry….. back into the freezer for at least 5 hours.

It's bake time

Place the tin onto a baking sheet for stability if you are using the silicone one and place into the middle of the oven for 25-30 mins.

Once baked, whilst the cookie is still soft use scissors to tidy the edges and remove any darker (overly cooked) bits.

Leave to cool, once cooled place into the fridge for again at least 6 hours.

(Do not put it in warm as this will affect the internal temperature of the fridge and possibly spoil the food that is in there)

Remove from the tin and slice into whatever size you would like. I drizzled mine with some of the remaining ganache, that I had saved and heated in the microwave.

Keep refrigerated until its time to eat, then remove an hour before eating.

xxxxxx

CALLEBAUT®
BELGIUM 1911

# OOZING BISCOFF COOKIES

## Ingredients

100g Melted Butter
60g Melted Biscoff, crunchy or smooth
75g Soft Brown Sugar
75g Caster Sugar
1 Large Egg
1 Tsp Vanilla
260g Plain Flour
20g Corn Flour
1/2 Tsp Bicarbonate of Soda
1 Tsp Baking Powder
150g Gold Chocolate Chips (We use Callebaut)
8 Tbsp Biscoff Spread for the filling

# Method

Scoop 8 1 Tbsp mound of Biscoff on to something lined that will fit in your freezer. This is to fill the cookie and will need to set firm to use, so do this in advance of the cookie dough. Once set they can be stored in a bag until you want to use them.

For the cookies;

Mix together the melted butter and Biscoff, add in the egg and Vanilla, and mix until it is smooth.

Add in the flour, corn flour, salt and raising agents and combine until almost mixed, then add in the chocolate chips. Mix until completely combined.

Using around 70g of the cookie mix and another 30g for the top. Add the frozen Biscoff to the top of the larger cookie mix and then add ontop the 30g piece, you need to encase the Biscoff with the dough.

Make up all 8 cookies and pop in the freezer to set up for at least 30 minutes.

Preheat the oven to 190C/170CFan375F/Gas5 bake straight from the freezer for 18 to 20 minutes.

When you bring them out of the oven give the tray a couple of sharp taps on the work surface, this will creat those lovely cracks on the top of the cookie.

# PEANUT CARAMEL COOKIE PIE

## Ingredients

225g Melted Butter
150g Caste Sugar
150g Soft Brown Sugar
1 large Egg
1 Egg Yolk
2 tsp Vanilla Extract
390g Plain Flour
30g Cornflour
3/4 tsp Bicarbonate of Soda
1 1/2 tsp Baking Powder
1/2 tsp slat
345g chocolate chips what ever combination you prefer.
4 peanut caramel chocolate bars

### Topping

150 g Melted Milk Chocolate
80g crunchy Peanut Butter
40g Honey
80g Caramel

CALLEBAUT
BELGIUM 1911

## Method

Preheat the oven to 190C/170CFan/375F/Gas5

Line an 8 inch tin around the sides and the base.

Mix together the melted butter, vanilla and the sugars, add in the egg and yolk and mix this up well. Then fold in all the dry ingredients until they are almost incorporated and add in the chocolate chips mix until you have no dry ingredients showing.

Evenly spread out half of the mix in the lined baking pan. Chop up the chocolate bars into 2 cm slices and lay them out over the cookie dough (you can add any chocolate bars that you like at this point). Cover with the rest of the cookie dough.

Pop into the oven for about 50 to 55 minutes. Ensure that the internal temperature reaches at least 72 degrees centigrade. You can check this from 48 minutes.

Allow to almost fully cool in the tin. Turn out of the tin.

Mix the melted chocolate and the peanut butter together, when mixed add in the honey and drizzle over the top of the cookie, drizzle the caramel over the top. And decorate with any chocolates you like, I used salted caramel buttons.

# BAKEWELL COOKIES

These are scrumptious Cookies that you wont be able to resit.

## Ingredients

100g Melted Butter
100g Caster Sugar
50g Light Brown Sugar
1 Large egg
1 tsp Vanilla Extract
1/4 tsp almond Extract
260g Plain Flour
20g Corn Flour
1 tsp Baking Powder
1/2 tsp Bicarbonate of Soda
1/4 tsp Salt
200g White Chocolate Chips
20g Freeze Dried Raspberries
Extra white choc chips and freeze dried raspberries for the top.

## Method

To make the cookie dough, add the sugars to the melted butter and mix together, beat in the egg, almond and vanilla until it is a smooth mix.

Add in the dry ingredients and mix by hand until almost incorporated, then add in the raspberries, chocolate chips and finish mixing, stop as soon as you all the flour is incorporated and the chocolate is evenly distributed.

Make into 12 cookies and chill for about 1 hour.

Bake at 190C/170CF/375F/Gas5 for 13 to 15 minutes.

Chill on the tray for about 5 minutes until moving to a cooling rack.

CALLEBAUT
BELGIUM 1911

# COCONUT & JAM BISCUITS

## Ingredients

150g Caster Sugar
175g Soft Butter
1 Egg & 1 Yolk
1/2 tbsp Coconut liquor (or 1/4 tsp
of coconut essence)
290g Plain Flour
30g Corn Flour
1/4 tsp Salt
70g Desiccated Coconut

For the Dip
2 tbs Caster Sugar
2 tbs Coconut
Combine these in a bowl.

Your favourite Jam, I like
Strawberry.

## Method

Preheat the oven to 190C/170CFan/375F/Gas5

Beat the sugar and butter together until light and fluffy.
Add in the egg and yolk and beat gently to combine.
Add in the Coconut flavour of your choice, mix and then pop all the dry ingredients in, beat on low until they are just combined.
Line a couple of cookie trays.

When the dough is combined, use a 2 tablespoon scoop for each biscuit, drop the biscuits in the coconut and sugar mixture and roll around. Make sure you have a ball so that it forms evenly.
Pop the coated biscuit ball on the baking sheet, using a 1/2 tablespoon measuring spoon, press into the centre of the cookie to make a well. If the spoon starts to get sticky, dip it in the sugar mix. Do this with all the biscuits until you have used the dough up.
Then pop 1/2 a teaspoon of jam in the centre.

Bake in the centre of the oven for 12 to 14 minutes, if you are baking 2 trays at one, swap them around at half time.
Allow to cool on the tray for 5 minutes and then transfer to a cooling rack.

# CHOCOLATE CHIP COOKIE BAR

## Ingredients

325g Plain Flour
20g Corn Flour
1 Tsp Bicarbonate of Soda
120g Light Muscavado Sugar
120g Dark Muscavado Sugar
200g Salted Butter
1 Lg Egg and 1 Egg Yolk
2 Tsp Vanilla Extract
200g Chocolate Chips (we
recommend Callebaut

**CALLEBAUT**
BELGIUM 1911

## Method

Fully line an 8" x 8" cake tin

Pre Heat your oven to 190C/170CFan/375F/Gas5

Place your butter into a bowl and melt this in the microwave, then add in the sugars and vanilla. Whilst this cools in a separate bowl mix together the flours, bicarb, salt and chocolate chips. Now the butter is cooler add in the eggs, give it a mix and then pour this over the dry ingredients.

Put this into your tin, but build it higher in the middle, like a small hill. We do this because the mix spreads and this will help it bake more evenly. It likes to creep up the sides!!

Bake for 30 to 35 mins. When you hit the tin it shouldn't wobble. Remove from the oven and allow it to cool for at least an hour. Now slice up and enjoy.

Add in your favourite chocolate treats to make this even yummier.

# CHOCOLATE & NUT COOKIE CLOUDS

## Ingredients

200g Egg Whites
450g Granulated Sugar
3/4 tsp Cream of Tartar
1 tbsp Vanilla Extract
140g chopped nuts. I used a mix of Pecan, hazelnut and sliced almonds.
200g Dark Chocolate Chips
Extra choc chips to top

## Method

Preheat the oven to 100 C Fan and line 2 large baking trays.

Most importantly, anything you are using must be super clean, I give mine a clean to be sure with lemon juice and kitchen towel, the bowl and the whisk and anything else I will use.
Put the egg whites, sugar and cream of tartar in a glass or metal bowl, I use the bowl from my mixer. ( it does cut down on washing up)

Use a saucepan big enough to sit the bowl you are using in and put about an inch of water in the bottom, you don't want the water to touch the bowl. Bring the pan of water to the boil and place the bowl of egg whites and sugar over it. (Like a bain-marie).

Cook this out whilst stirring, when all of the sugar is dissolved (rub the mixture in your fingers, if you can't feel any sugar granules you are good to go).
Take this to your mixer, and with a whisk attachment, whisk until thick, glossy and has supper sharp peaks and it is not too hot, you don't want to melt the chocolate.

Tip in the nuts and chocolate chips, fold into the mixture.
Using a large ice cream scoop, scoop the mixture onto the lined trays, they don't spread too much but leave an inch between each.
Top each one with a sprinkle of chocolate chips.

Place in the oven, one tray in the centre and the next below. Straight away turn the oven to 140 C Fan and cook for 1 hour switching the trays around half way through cooking.

Leave to cool in the oven with the door cranked for 1 hour after baking, you can take them out straight away but they will be a little chewier.

# BISCOFF CHEESECAKE COOKIE CUPS

## Ingredients

### Cookie dough

150g Melted Butter
75g Caster Sugar
75g Light Brown Sugar
1 Large egg
1 tsp Vanilla Extract
260g Plain Flour
20g Corn Flour
1 tsp Baking Powder
1/2 tsp Bicarbonate of Soda
1/4 tsp Salt
100g White Chocolate Chips
100g Milk Chocolate Chips

### Biscoff cheesecake

175g Biscoff Spread, smooth or crunchy.
380g Full fat Cream Cheese
70g Caster Sugar
35g Double Cream
1 tsp Corn Flour
2 Large Eggs

## Method

Oven Temp 190C/170CFan/375F/Gas5
To make the cookie dough, add the sugars to the melted butter and mix together, beat in the egg and vanilla until it is a smooth mix. Add in the dry ingredients and mix by hand until almost incorporated, then add in the chocolate chips and finish mixing, stop as soon as you all the flour is incorporated and the chocolate is evenly distributed.

Weigh out 90g balls of cookie dough and pop into a muffin tin, you can line this with one strip of parchment about an inch wide and so that you have plenty free at the top to help pull the cookie out, using a shot glass push the dough down so that it is in a cup shape, and the tops reach the top of the muffin tin.
For the cheesecake mix, mix together the Biscoff spread, if its tough warm for a few seconds in the microwave, the cream cheese, sugar, and double cream. Once all mixed together add in both eggs and the corn flour, whisk until smooth and fully incorporated.

Pour in the cheesecake mix until almost to the top and bake in the centre of the oven for 18 mins, you should still have a wobble on the cheesecake when it comes out. Cool completely in the tin and the pop in the fridge for a couple of hours or until the cookie will release. Top
with Biscoff spread.

Or if you want to make cookie cups and fill after baking, repeat the process but don't fill with cheesecake, bake for 14 minutes and as soon as they come out of the oven, repeat the process with the shot glass and press the centre of the baked cookie down, chill in the tin before turning out.

# VIENNESE SWIRLS

## Ingredients

350g Very Soft Butter
100g Icing Sugar
370g Plain Flour
50g Corn Flour
1/4 tsp Salt
1 tsp Vanilla

Extra icing sugar to dust
Strawberry Jam
Half a batch of Connors
Buttercream Silk *page 146*

## Method

Preheat the oven to 180C/160CFan/350F/Gas4

Line 2 baking Trays and fit a very strong piping bag with a 356 piping tip, be sure to cut away as little of the bag as possible if using a disposable one, this makes a very dense mixture and needs strength in the bag to hold up.

In a stand mixer with a paddle attachment, beat the butter and icing sugar together until it is smooth and pale, mix in the vanilla.

Then add in the dry ingredients and mix just until the dough comes together.

Transfer half to the piping bag, and pipe rosettes onto your baking tray. Using half the mixture at a time is easier to handle, you need to be very firm with the bag and unlike buttercream the warmth from your hand helps, I hold mine right to the tip, not only for warmth but to support the tip from bursting out. You should get 28 cookies, depending on the size you pipe.

Bake in the oven for 14 minutes rotating the trays half way through.

When they are baked allow them to cool for about 5 minutes on the trays then gently transfer to a rack.

When they are cool, match up 2 of the same size and fill with a ring of Connors buttercream Silk and a small spoon of strawberry jam in the centre. Place them together as a sandwich and dust with icing sugar.

# JO'S
# STRAWBERRY SHORTCAKE

## Ingredients

220g Cold butter Cubbed
380g Plain Flour
40g Corn Flour
70g Caster Sugar
1 1/2 tsp Baking Powder
1/2 tsp Bicarbonate of Soda
1/2 tsp salt
240g Buttermilk
Pear Sugar to sprinkle

### Filling
A good quality strawberry jam we
recommend **Wexford Home Preserves**
300g strawberries
4 tbsp Pimms
2 tbsp Sugar

## Method

Begin by whipping up a large tub of cream, you can sweeten it if you like.

Preheat the oven to 210 Fan Centigrade.

Hull and slice your strawberries and macerate with the Pimms and sugar for a minimum of 30 minutes.

Put all the dry ingredients into a large bowl and rub in the cold butter until you have breadcrumbs and a few small pea sized lumps.

Using a pallet knife or you hand in a claw, add in the buttermilk, you may not need it all depending on the humidity. You want a wet sticky mix with no dry parts. Do not knead the dough.

On 2 lined trays separate the mix into 12 rough balls of equal sizes with floured fingers. This will not be a smooth mix.
Sprinkle Pearl sugar over the top of each shortcake and bake rotating the shelves at half time for 13 to 16 minutes.

Cool and split in half, pop the jam on then the cream, then dress with the macerated strawberries and drizzle with a little of the syrup.

# BILLIONAIRE'S STICKY TOFFEE SHORTBREAD

## Ingredients

**Shortbread**
175g Soft Butter
150g Caster Sugar
1 egg 1 yolk
1 tbsn Golden Syrup
1/2 tsp Salt
1 tsp Vanilla extract
360g Plain Flour
30g Corn Flour

150g Butter
170g Caster Sugar
150g Light Brown Sugar
150g Double Cream

400g of milk chocolate
200g double cream

CALLEBAUT®
BELGIUM 1911

## Method

Beat together butter and sugar until light and fluffy, add in the eggs, vanilla and syrup and beat in gently. Then pop the flours into the mix and again gently mix until incorporated, do not over mix.

Tip the dough out onto your work surface and lightly knead together, pushing it away from you and pulling it back until smooth. This will only be for a minute, do not overwork the dough.

Use 3/4 of the mix to line a 10 inch square tin, chill for 20 minutes in the fridge and bake at 170C/150CFan/325F/Gas3 for 27 minutes.

To make the Sticky toffee caramel.
Melt the butter add in the caster sugar and light brown sugar and bring to a boil to about 110c then and add in the double cream and boil to 115c.
Add in a teaspoon of salt and teaspoon of vanilla and spoon over the cooked shortbread then chill.

To make the chocolate ganache
Bring the double cream to gentle boil and then pour over the chocolate, give a little mix and leave for a minute. Then gently stir until all the chocolate is melted.
Pour the Ganache over the chilled caramel and decorate, you can use the
use the chilled leftover shortbread dough to make shapes to top. The little stars baked at 150 c for 6 minutes.

Decorate with lots of bling for the party season.

# SQUIRLY WHIRLY COOKIES

## Ingredients

### Cookie dough

150g Melted Butter
50g Caster Sugar
100g Light Brown Sugar
1 Large egg
1 tsp Vanilla Extract
240g Plain Flour
20g Corn Flour
20g Cocoa Powder
1 tsp Baking Powder
1/2 tsp Bicarbonate of Soda
1/4 tsp Salt
50g White Chocolate Chips
100g Milk Chocolate Chips
90g Squirly Whirly Wiggles Chocolate

Extra Squirly Whirly wiggles Chocolate to top

## Method

To make the cookie dough, add the sugars to the melted butter and mix together, beat in the egg and vanilla until it is a smooth mix.

Add in the dry ingredients and mix by hand until almost incorporated, then add in the chocolate chips and Squirlies and finish mixing, stop as soon as all the flour is incorporated and the chocolate is evenly distributed.

With a large ice cream scoop, make cookie mounds, chill or freeze for an hour.

Bake at 190C/170CFan/375F/Gas5 for 14 minutes, as soon as they come out of the oven use a large cookie cutter to swirl the cookie around as the caramel from the chocolate try's to escape, this will also give each cookie a lovely uniformed shape, top with extra whirlies.

CALLEBAUT®
BELGIUM 1911

# After Dinner Treats

# JINNY'S BOURBON BISCUIT CHEESECAKE

## Ingredients

Use an 8 inch fully lined spring form cake tin

450g Bourbon Biscuits

160g Melted Unsalted Butter

200g Double Cream

450g Philadelphia Full Fat Cream Cheese ( this brand works the best as it has less water content, you may not get the same structure with another brand)

150g Melted Chocolate ( we recommend Callebaut Milk Chocolate 823)

2 Tbsp Cocoa Powder ( we use the Callebaut Cocoa Plein Arome)

50 to 100g Icing Sugar (for a sweeter cheesecake add the 100g. I used 50g for the more traditional cheesecake taste)

1 tsp Vanilla Extract

1/4 tsp Coffee, dissolve this into the vanilla

1 Tsp Lemon Juice

Pinch of Salt

For the Topping

260g Milk Chocolate ( again we recommend Callebaut 823)

170g Double Cream

# Method

## To make the base

Separate the filling from the biscuit. Snap the bourbon open and with a knife scrape the filling into a bowl. Keep the biscuit and the filling separate. Pop the filling to one side for later.

Crush the biscuits by either placing them in a ziplock bag and giving them a good old bash, or pop them into a mixer. You can have them like breadcrumbs or a little more textured its up to you. Melt the butter and mix into the biscuit crumb.

Into your lined tin (sides too) pour in the mix and push it all down to form an even level. I find using a potato masher is great, it compacts it in and helps with a level coating. Pop into the fridge.

## Let's move onto the filling.

Pour your cold cream into the mixer and turn it on low, using the balloon whisk, as it is going add 1 tsp lemon juice to it. Jo taught me this and it works....even though I didn't believe her!!!! It helps the mixture to set ( who knew!! I hate it when she is right!) Turn up the speed, just as you see it thickening and forming soft ribbons....STOP. We don't want curdled cream and this happens in an instant. If you do go to far try adding some more cream to it and gently folding it in.

To this now pour in the cream cheese, as this is whipping, melt your chocolate and the bourbon filling, that you left to one side earlier. Whip the cream cheese/cream for around 2-3 mins on medium/high. Once the chocolate and the bourbon mixture has cooled slightly, add this into the mix along with the cocoa powder, icing sugar, vanilla/coffee mix and the salt. Whip until fully combined, ensuring you scrape down. The mixture should be a thick consistency.

Take the tin out of the fridge and pour this over the crumb base, try not to eat it as you go!!!!!! Level it off, I find using the back of a spoon is helpful. Return this to the fridge for at least 6 hours.

To make the topping, we are going to make a ganache.

Pour your cream over the chocolate in a microwave proof bowl and pop into the microwave. Melt this in short bursts, it should take around 1 min to melt but do this in 3 stages, stirring each time. If you heat it too fast, for too long, the chocolate may seize which will result in the fats coming out. Allow this to cool to around 20-22C/68F-71F then pour it over the "set" cheesecake filling. Leave it longer if it isn't firm to the touch.

Return it again to the fridge for a few more hours. It may seem set but the flavours develop over about 8 hours.

EAT TIME..... remove the spring form and then gently peel the parchment from the sides. Decorate anyway you wish and enjoy xxxxxx

* I used a 2E nozzle for my decoration

# JO'S BISCOFF CHEESECAKE

## Ingredients

100g Digestive Biscuits
6 Biscoff Cream filled biscuits
50g melted Butter

175g Smooth Biscoff spread
380g Cream Cheese
70g Caster Sugar
35g Double Cream
1 tsp Corn Flour
2 Large Eggs

80g Biscoff Spread

## Method

Preheat the oven to 180C/160CFan/350F/Gas4.
Line the base and sides of a 6 inch loose bottom pan.

Crush all of the biscuits and then mix in the melted butter, Press the crumb into the base of the lined pan, use a flat bottomed tumbler to make it nice and compact.
Bake in the centre of the oven for 10 minutes.

Meanwhile cream together the Biscoff, cream cheese, sugar and cornflour. Then whisk in the eggs and double cream.
Pour this into the baked base and pop back into the oven on the middle shelf.

Bake for 50 to 55 minutes, the top needs to look set but the middle should still have a little wiggle, Don't worry about any cracks.

Leave to cool in the tin on a cooling rack, once cool enough place in the fridge and allow to chill for a few hours or overnight.

Ensure that the sides are free from the tin and slide the base up to remove the cheesecake, Remove the lining. Warm the Biscoff a little in the microwave to ensure that it spreads easily and top the cheesecake.

Slice with a clean hot knife to get clean cuts.

# PLUM COBBLER

## Ingredients

115g Cold Butter
190g Plain Flour
20g Cornflour
3/4 tsp Baking Powder
1/4 tsp Bicarbonate of Soda
50g Sugar
1/2 tsp Salt
135g Natural Yoghurt
1 tsp Ground Ginger
20g Toasted slithered Almonds
A little extra sugar for the top

700g halved and stoned plums
100 frozen blackberries
Juice and zest of 1 lemon
100g Sugar
50g toasted slithered almonds

## Method

Preheat the oven to
200C/180CFan/400F/Gas6

In a 9 x 7 inch pie dish, put the halved and stoned plums, blackberries and sugar in along with the zest of the lemon and squeeze in all of the juice, mix this so that it is evenly distributed and sprinkle the almonds over the top.

Put all the dry ingredients into a large bowl and rub in the cold butter until you have breadcrumbs and a few small pea sized lumps.

Using a pallet knife or you hand in a claw, add in the yoghurt. You want a wet sticky mix with no dry parts. Do not knead the dough.

With floured fingers break off chunks of the cobbler mix and drop it evenly over the fruit, I got about 9 pieces from it. Sprinkle with a little sugar and the Almond slithers.

Bake for 45 to 50 minutes, until the top is golden and fruit is bubbling.
Serve with fresh cream, ice cream or custard.

# ULTIMATE CARAMEL CHEESECAKE

## Ingredients

150g Crushed Digestive Biscuits
90g Browned Butter
1 tbsp Light Brown Sugar

160g Tinned Caramel
150g Full fat Cream Cheese
250g Mascarpone
45g Caster Sugar
15g Light Brown Sugar
50g Double Cream
1 tsp Plain Flour
2 Large Eggs

Extra Caramel to top

## Method

Preheat the oven to 180C/160CFan/350F/Gas4
Line the base and sides of a 6 inch loose bottom tin.

Pop the butter into a small pan and cook until it foams up and becomes a lovely straw brown colour and smells nutty.

Mix the Crushed biscuits, sugar and Brown butter together and press into the bottom of the prepared pan. I use the bottom of a tumble to get a neat base.

Bake in the oven for 10 minutes.

For the cheesecake mix, mix together the caramel , (warm if its thick), mascarpone, the cream cheese, sugars, and double cream. Once all mixed together add in both eggs and the flour, whisk until smooth and fully incorporated.

Pour into the tin, over the top of the biscuit base and bake in the centre of the oven for 1 hour. You will still have a slight wobble, crank the oven door open and allow to cool in the turned off oven for about 30 minutes. Chill completely and then refrigerate preferably overnight.
Warm the sides of the tin to release, I use my hands und gently run a knife around.

Top with a generous amount of warmed caramel, slice with a clean hot knife.

# CHOCOLATE TRUFFLES

These are super simple and very cute, if you are making these for the chocolate truffle cup cakes, you will need about 25g balls to use, follow the recipe and coat in cocoa powder.

## Ingredients

200g Double Cream
400g Milk for Dark Chocolate
40g Cocoa Powder

## Method

Heat the cream to a low boil, I use the microwave, you want to see steam and a few bubbles.

Add the chocolate straight into the cream, give a little stir and set aside for a minute.

Stir again gently until all the chocolate is melted. Set aside to cool and then chill in the fridge for half an hour.

Pop the sieved cocoa powder into a bowl and scoop out tablespoons of the ganache, roll into a ball and drop in the cocoa powder. Roll around until covered, or you can dip them in melted chocolate and decorate with nuts for a more indulgent flavour.

# BUTTERCREAMS

We call each of these recipes 1 batch. This is enough to cover 12 cupcakes, with a standard swirl. It will also cover a 2 layer cake. then just multiply by how many layers you need.

## Salted vs Unsalted

Love this one, it's always guaranteed to get a group of bakers chatting!!! So what is the answer!!! We say there isn't one, you choose. Some prefer the sweetness of icing sugar, so use unsalted butter, to not detract from the flavour. Some prefer to use half and half, just taking the edge off the sweetness. Then there's fully salted butter, this will pull the sweetness right down, we find this is best used when you have another flavour, like chocolate, peanut butter etc. Do some test batches and see what your preference is.

If you want to control the level of salt yourself, just use unsalted butter and beginning with 1/8 tsp add until you have the desired flavour.

## What is the benefit of Connors Buttercream vs Regular

So we hear "it's just melting butter isn't"?

Well thats kind of right but also very misleading. When you melt butter over 30C, the structure changes and it separates, using this will affect your buttercream. the split layer will float on the top!!

So by cutting the butter into cubes and microwaving in very small bursts, we control the temperature, never letting it go above 30C. This brings it to a lovely consistency, it takes on the sieved icing sugar well and allows it to dissolve slightly, removing some of that gritty texture.

The second part is because it soaks in so well, there is not need to WHIP & WHIP the buttercream, which causes all of those air pockets we spend ages trying to get rid of. Just mixing it in on low for a very short time, or combing by hand (spatula not literally hands!!!) leaves a super smooth, flawless buttercream with a lovely texture. It is so quick to make as well you will be ready to go in just 5 mins.

## Deep Coloured Buttercream

Using the Connor's method, this works so well. Place your colouring on the top of the butter (we recommend our "Simply Colours" range) Then continue to make Connors in the regular way. Due to not whipping the buttercream, we are not reducing the intensity of the colour.

For an even deeper colour, use an emersion blender.

# Buttercreams & Flavourings

# SALTED CARAMEL

## Ingredients

500g White Sugar

200g Salted Butter

200g Double Cream

1 tsp Vanilla Extract

½ tsp Salt ** optional

for the salted caramel

## Method

To begin you need to use a saucepan with a wide bottom, we want the sugar to only have a thin layer. Using a smaller pan will mean the sugar has a thick coating and the bottom is more likely to burn before the heat reaches the top.

Pour your sugar into the pan and put this on a medium heat, don't go too high too quickly or it will burn. Every minute swirl the pan around, do not add any utensils into this or it will cause crystallisation, which means sugar lumps. You will see that the outer parts start to melt and become an amber colour, continuing to swirl often. Taking it off the heat to swirl will help the bottom to not burn. The more the sugar melts, try to keep it off the heat for about 10 seconds at a time, this will give the top layer a chance to incorporate with the bottom and melt. You want to keep the amber colour not turn into a deeper brown as this will make the caramel bitter, you will be able to smell it if it has become too hot and burnt.
I took mine off the heat for the last minute and it did eventually dissolve, the bottom sugar is very hot.

Once it has all melted add in your butter, but do this in chunks and stir it in, be very careful as it will bubble up slightly. If it looks as though it is struggling to incorporate, pop it back onto the heat, but not for long. I like to have the pan half on and half off the ring, but I have an electric stove so this is possible.

Once it is all incorporated and silky add in the cream and salt if you are doing salted caramel, this does bubble a lot so do it at an arm's length. Stir it in and then add the vanilla. Pop it into a separate bowl and cover with cling. Once cooled, store it in the fridge.

# TOFFEE SAUCE

## Ingredients

220g Dark Brown Sugar

200g Salted Butter

110g Double Cream

½ tsp Vanilla Extract

## Method

In a large saucepan add the sugar, butter and cream all together and place on a medium heat. Do not stir at this point, you can swirl the pan so that the temperature evenly distributes, but adding utensils before the mix dissolves can cause crystallisation.

Once the butter melts and you can see the sugar has dissolved, increase to a medium high heat and begin to stir. Continue to stir until it becomes thicker and covers the back of a spoon with a silky layer, then add the Vanilla.

Once it is done, cover with cling film and leave on the side to cool, it can then be placed in the fridge. If it is too thick when you need it, just give it a very quick ping in the microwave. Be careful it heats very fast and will burn easily.

Use this for sticky toffee pudding, in ganache over buttercream or just dip your finger in it and enjoy. Don't tell the dentist!!!

# LIME CURD

## Ingredients

6 Limes Zested
4 Limes Juiced
210g Sugar
3 Egg Yolks
1 Egg
120g Cold Butte

## Method

Add all your ingredients to a bowl except the butter and set a pan of water on the heat, whisk the Lime mix together and set over the pan, this only needs to be simmering and the water should not be touching the bottom of the bowl. With a whisk keep the mixture moving, it doesn't need to be heavily whisked but needs to be moved around, if the heat is gentle, you will be fine. This process can take up to 20 minutes so be patient, it is so worth it.

When you have a thick mix, and you can leave lines or ribbons over the surface you are ready to take it from the heat.

Sieve into a bowl and add in the soft butter a little at a time until incorporated, transfer the curd to sterilised jars or use it in a dessert.

To Keep

To sterilise, place the clean jars and lids into a large pan and cover with water, bring to a boil and boil for to minutes, keep them in the hot water until you are ready to decant your jam. I use tongs to remove the jars and a clean towel to hold them whilst tightening the lids.

# BLUEBERRY JAM

This is great with the pound cake.

## Ingredients

150g Frozen Blueberries
90g Granulated Sugar
Juice of 1/2 lemon
Case of 1/2 a lemon

## Method

Pop all of the ingredients in a pan and bring to a boil, stirring often. (Make sur that you have removed all the pips from the lemon)

When it is good and bubbly, go in with a potato masher and crush all of the blueberries, give the lemon a little squish too.

With a cold plate, place a little bit of the mix on and allow it to cool, test to see if it is the thickness you want, if its still a little thin boil a bit longer. About 10 minutes should be good, depending on the heat you are using.

When it is ready discard the lemon and decant into a sterilised jar, or bowl if you are using straight away.

# FRUIT 'STUFF'

## Ingredients

Any frozen bag of berries, I do a few bags at a time as it all freezes so well. If you store them in ice cube trays you just need to pop out a cube when you need one.

This "stuff" is a completely natural intense fruit reduction, that brings an intense flavour to your bakes and buttercreams. It will work with any berry as they reduce so well and have a high water content.

I use frozen berries as there is no waste and there is no need to add any more liquid.

## Method

Empty your fruit into a saucepan and turn the heat up to high until some of the ice melts. Keep stirring periodically through this process as if it burns the whole batch is ruined.

Once the berries have started to release some liquid turn the heat down to medium and allow this to simmer away for around 10 mins. Don't forget to stir every min, scraping the bottom well each time.

As the liquid boils off the fruit will get thicker and thicker, when it starts to look like there is no more water keep stirring as this is the time it can ruin.

We are looking for this to become a very thick paste, almost gluey. You will know it is done when it no longer bubbles and the "stuff" sticks together pulling away from the bottom of the pan when you stir it. Pour this mix into a bowl and cover with cling until it has cooled.

If you have used a berry with a lot of seeds whilst it is warm, not hot, push it through a sieve repeatedly and using a clean spoon scrape the paste off the back of the sieve. When all you have left is seeds it is all done.

This is now a massively concentrated fruit paste, the flavour carries such a punch that you don't need much at all. The beauty of this is that there are no additives; it is just a pure, intense flavour.

# STRAWBERRY JAM

## Ingredients

1 KG of Fresh strawberries

800g Jam Sugar

## Method

Hull (core them) the strawberries and place them into a large pan with the sugar.

Using a potato masher gives them a good crush and set the pan on a medium heat. Simmer until the mix has become liquid and turn the heat up a little to get a rolling boil (make sure the pan is large enough as this will raise up quite high and it can get very messy).

I keep a saucer in the fridge to test the jam, on the cold saucer drop a teaspoon of the jam and pop it back in the fridge for 10 seconds. Bring it out of the fridge and push the edge of the jam to the middle, if it wrinkles and looks set then it's good to go.

Skim off any froth from the top and discard.

I use a large Kilner jar or smaller jam jars. To sterilise, place the clean jars and lids into a large pan and cover with water, bring to a boil and boil for 10 minutes, keep them in the hot water until you are ready to decant your jam. I use tongs to remove the jars and a clean towel to hold them whilst tightening the lids.

### TOP TIP
If you don't have any jam sugar, use a whole lemon rind in the mix from the start and discard at the end, or a grated eating apple with the skin on.

# CREAM CHEESE FROSTING

## Ingredients

465g Icing Sugar
1/4 tsp salt
75g Soft Butter
3/4 tsp Vanilla Extract
180g Cream Cheese

## Method

To make the cream cheese frosting, sift the icing sugar into the bowl of a stand mixer with the paddle attachment on, add in the soft butter. On low, mix this until you have a light breadcrumb texture, clean down the paddle and bowl to ensure there is no butter left.

Add in the cream cheese, salt and vanilla and mix on low until almost incorporated and scrape down. Turn the mixer to medium and beat until smooth.

# CONNOR'S BUTTERCREAM SILK

## Ingredients

250g Block Butter (Salted Unsalted or half and half, your choice)
500g Sieved Icing Sugar
1 Tsp Milk Powder
2 Tsp Vanilla Extract

## Method

Cube your butter up into small squares. You can do this from the fridge or room temp butter. The harder the butter the more time it will need in the microwave. This is a guide, if it is not completely firm or room temp, just do something in between.

### From Hard

15 seconds in the microwave, then stir
then a further 10 seconds, stir again
If it is not ready only use 5 second bursts now.

### From Soft

5 seconds in the microwave, then stir
then, further 5 second bursts until it is ready.
You are looking for the butter to be no hotter than 30C/84F, the butter should look the consistency and colour of thick custard. It should not turn florescent, if it does just keep stirring until it comes under 30C and has that creamy look.
Add the sieved icing sugar, you can do this by hand in a bowl or on the mixer.

### By Hand

Add the sugar, milk powder and optional invert sugar over the butter and cut through until it is mostly combined.
**Then using the back of the spatula push backward and forwards into the buttercream to smooth it out. This will also push the butter and icing sugar all together. Once it has become very smooth it is ready.
(Use this for the second part of the Mixer method too)

## Mixer

Add the sugar, milk powder, and butter into the bowl and using the paddle mixer on LOW, allow the mixer to partially combine the two. There should be some faint hints of icing sugar around the edges of the buttercream. If you combine it too much, air will begin to be pushed into the mix, causing those pesky bubbles!!!! The mixer should not be on longer than 40 seconds.
Now use the spatula like above** to make it all come together.

If it is too thick add 1-2 Tbsn Milk/Water

# FLAVOURED CONNOR'S BUTTERCREAM SILK

## Ingredients

250g Block Butter (Salted Unsalted or half and half, your choice)
500g Sieved Icing Sugar
1 Tsp Milk Powder
1 Tsp Vanilla
Flavouring from below

## Flavourings

### Lemon
2 Tbsp Lemon Curd
Zest of 2 lemons added to your sugar and left overnight.

### Strawberry
2 Tbsn "Strawberry Stuff" page 142

### Toffee
2 Tbsn Toffee Sauce page 139

### Nutella
100g Nutella
2 Tbsn Cocoa Powder added to the icing sugar

### Biscoff
50g Biscoff

### Salted Caramel
2 Tbsn Salted Caramel page 138

### White Chocolate
120g Melted White Chocolate, we use Callebaut W2 White Chocolate

### Coffee
1 Tsp Coffee mixed in 2 Tbsp milk

### Chocolate Orange
2 Tbsp Cocoa Powder mixed with 2 Tbsp orange juice and the zest of an orange

### Peanut Butter
2 Tbsp smooth peanut butter, mixed with 3 tbsp milk

# FLAVOURED CONNOR'S BUTTERCREAM SILK

## Method

Cube your butter up into small squares. You can do this from the fridge or room temp butter. The harder the butter the more time it will need in the microwave. This is a guide, if it is not completely firm or room temp, just do something in between.

### From Hard

15 seconds in the microwave, then stir
then a further 10 seconds, stir again
If it is not ready only use 5 second bursts now.

### From Soft

5 seconds in the microwave, then stir
then, further 5 second bursts until it is ready.
You are looking for the butter to be no hotter than 30C/84F, the butter should look the consistency and colour of thick custard. It should not turn florescent, if it does just keep stirring until it comes under 30C and has that creamy look.
Add the sieved icing sugar, you can do this by hand in a bowl or on the mixer.

### By Hand

Add the sugar, milk powder, FLAVOURING and the butter and cut through until it is mostly combined.
**Then using the back of the spatula push backward and forwards into the buttercream to smooth it out. This will also push the butter and icing sugar all together. Once it has become very smooth it is ready.
(Use this for the second part of the Mixer method too)

### Mixer

Add the sugar, milk powder, FLAVOURING and butter into the bowl and using the paddle mixer on LOW, allow the mixer to partially combine the two. There should be some faint hints of icing sugar around the edges of the buttercream. If you combine it too much, air will begin to be pushed into the mix, causing those pesky bubbles!!!!
The mixer should not be on longer than 40 seconds.
Now use the spatula like above** to make it all come together.

# CONNORS CHOCOLATE BUTTERCREAM

## Ingredients

250g Butter (You can use half salted and half unsalted to cut down the sweetness)

125g Callebaut Milk Chocolate (You can use White, Plain, Gold or Ruby Chocolate with the same ratios)

500g Icing Sugar

1tsp Vanilla

1tbsp Cocoa Powder (Optional, this is for a more intense chocolate taste)

## Method

Place your butter into a microwave-safe bowl and heat for around a minute in bursts until melted but still shows some lumps of butter (the temperature of the butter MUST not go above 30C as this will cause the butter to split).

In a separate bowl melt you chocolate and when slightly cool add it into the butter

Add the cocoa powder to the icing sugar,

Mix this into the butter/choc mixture by hand until its all incorporated and silky, pour in the vanilla and add boiling water if needed.

Use immediately or store it in the fridge.

# MOCK CREAM CHEESE FROSTING

## Ingredients

500g Icing Sugar
250g Block Butter
( salted or unsalted for your taste)

1 ½  tsp cider/white
wine vinegar
½ tsp milk
½ tsp lemon
¼ tsp milk powder
¼ tsp salt
1 tsp Vanilla

## Method

Begin by mixing the Mock solution together.

"Mock Solution"
In a bowl add the vinegar, milk, lemon, milk powder and salt together and set to the side.

Place your butter into a microwave safe bowl and heat in short bursts until its mostly melted, but still shows some lumps of butter (the temperature of the butter MUST not go above 30C as this will cause the butter to split).

Add in the "mock solution", vanilla and the sieved icing sugar. Mix this up using the paddle attachment on low, or by hand until its all incorporated and silky.
It is now ready to use and will be beautifully silky smooth. Add boiling water if needed.

To colour we recommend putting the colouring into the butter before melting.

# STABILISED WHIPPED CREAM

No gelatine required for this moorish recipe, this cream tastes like it has just come out of your favourite bakery. Be warned one spoonful is never enough and certainly not diet friendly. The milk powder is the stabiliser for this recipe.

## Ingredients

600g Super Cold Double Cream
125g sifted Icing Sugar
18g Milk Powder
1 tbsp Vanilla Extract

## Method

Chill your mixing bowl in the fridge for 20 minutes before starting this process.

With the whisk attachment fitted to your stand mixer, and a cold bowl add in all of the ingredients.

Whip on medium until you see it start to leave fine lines in the cream. Stop and scrape down ensuring all the ingredients have come together and whip again, this will stiffen fast, so be extra vigilant DO NOT WALK AWAY (unless you want sweet butter).

When you see it start to thicken and when you lift the whisk you have soft peaks, Stop.

You can mix a little more by hand, but remember every time you move the cream, with a spatula to fill a piping bag or to spoon on, this will keep agitating the mix and continue to thicken. If you think it has gone a little too far and is looking slightly split, stir in a little cold double cream, this can bring it back if it hasn't gone too far.

# MERINGUE FROSTING

Our Version of the 7 minute frosting, this is so nice to use and pipe's beautifully, its messy so be warned, but once you've tried it you wont look back. Goes perfectly with our Pineapple and Coconut Cake.

## Ingredients

200g Egg Whites
450g Granulated Sugar
3/4 tsp Cream of Tartar
1 tbsp Vanilla Extract

## Method

Most important, anything you are using must be super clean, I give mine a clean to be sure with lemon juice and kitchen towel, the bowl and the whisk and anything else I will use.

Put the egg whites, sugar and cream of tartar in a glass or metal bowl, I use the bowl from my mixer.

Use a saucepan big enough to sit the bowl you are using in and put about an inch of water in the bottom, you don't want the water to touch the bowl.

Bring the pan of water to the boil and place the bowl of egg whites and sugar over it. (Like a bain-marie).

You will need a thermometer, stirring constantly bring the mix up to at least 71 degrees Centigrade. Transfer straight to the stand mixer and whisk until the mixture is thick, glossy, has stiff peaks
This should take on high speed, about 7 minutes.

You need to use this frosting straight away (you have about an hour if it is covered) as it has a natural set, I have covered a cake in it and also Piped on top of our Lime Meringue Cupcakes.

On a cake you can go for the rustic look, think of Artex on the walls in the 80's. Also it is great torched with a kitchen torch and tastes like toasted Marshmallows.
Hope you love it like we do.

# SWISS MERINGUE BUTTERCREAM

This buttercream is lovely, sweet and melt in the mouth. It smooths on a cake beautifully and pipes like a dream.

## Ingredients

200g Egg Whites
450g Granulated Sugar
3/4 tsp Cream of Tartar
1 tbsp Vanilla Extract
500g Soft Butter (pre whipped butter will make this easier)

## Method

Most important anything you are using before adding the butter must be super clean, I give mine a clean to be sure with lemon juice and kitchen towel, the bowl and the whisk and anything else I will use.

Put the egg whites, sugar and cream of tartar in a glass or metal bowl, I use the bowl from my mixer. (But this does take longer to cool to temperature, it does cut down on washing up)

Use a saucepan big enough to sit the bowl you are using in and put about an inch of water in the bottom, you don't want the water to touch the bowl.

Bring the pan of water to the boil and place the bowl of egg whites and sugar over it. (Like a bain-marie).

You will need a thermometer, stirring constantly bring the mix up to at least 71 degrees Centigrade. Transfer straight to the stand mixer and whisk until the mixture is thick, glossy, has stiff peaks and is down to at least 22 degrees centigrade.

Start to add the butter a little at a time, don't add the next piece of butter until the last is unseen. When you have added all the butter keep whisking until you see the mixture start to pull away from the sides and look very thick and glossy.

If you get a soupy mix then your meringue was too warm when you started, don't worry, chill the mix for a few minutes and whip again, it will all come together.

# MOCHA BUTTERCREAM

## Ingredients

250g Butter
500g Icing Sugar
1/8 Salt (leave out if using salted butter)
1-2 Tsp Coffee Powder (to your taste)
2 Tbsp Cocoa Powder
1 Tsp Vanilla Extract
3-4 Tbsp milk

## Method

Cube your butter up into small squares. You can do this from the fridge or room temp butter. The harder the butter the more time it will need in the microwave. This is a guide, if it is not completely firm or room temp, just do something in between.

**From Hard**

15 seconds in the microwave, then stir
then a further 10 seconds, stir again
If it is not ready only use 5 second bursts now.

**From Soft**

5 seconds in the microwave, then stir
then, further 5 second bursts until it is ready.
You are looking for the butter to be no hotter than 30C/84F, the butter should look the consistency and colour of thick custard. It should not turn florescent, if it does just keep stirring until it comes under 30C and has that creamy look.
Add the sieved icing sugar, cocoa powder, coffee powder (mixed with the milk) and vanilla, you can mix this by hand in a bowl or on the mixer

**Mixer**

Using the paddle mixer on LOW, allow the mixer to partially combine the ingredients. There should be some faint hints of icing sugar around the edges of the buttercream. If you combine it too much, air will begin to be pushed into the mix, causing those pesky bubbles!!!! The mixer should not be on longer than 40 seconds.
Now use the spatula like below** to make it all come together.

**By Hand**

Add the sugar, cocoa powder, coffee powder (mixed with the milk) and vanilla, over the butter and cut through until it is mostly combined.
**Then using the back of the spatula push backward and forwards into the buttercream to smooth it out. This will also push the butter and icing sugar all together. Once it has become very smooth it is ready.
(Use this for the second part of the Mixer method too)

# RICE KRISPY TREATS FOR SCULPTING

## Ingredients

130g marshmallows
65g White chocolate
100 g Mambra Puffed Rice

## Method

Melt the marshmallows until puffed up and add in the puffed rice, mix together with a spatula, this will be very sticky. Add in the melted white chocolate and mix until you can't. Get your hands in there, it will stick at first but the fats in the chocolate will soon get the sticky stuff from your hands. Then you need to knead this until the chocolate is incorporated. Shape the model to your preference and then compact the treat until you are not able to add any further pressure. Once cool this will be solid and good to go. To reform any remaining just heat for a few seconds at a time until you can model the treats.

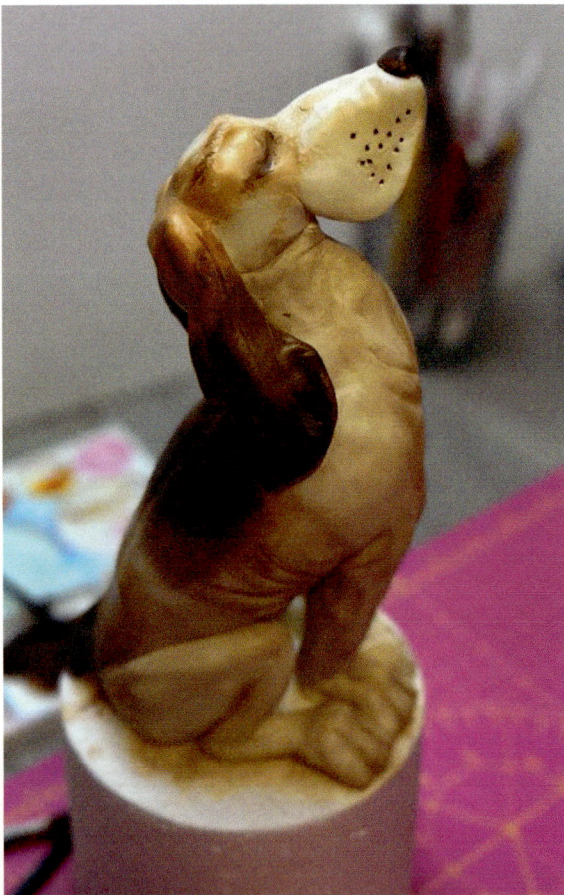

# INDEX